ECOTOURISM

ECOTOURISM

B.S. Badan
Harish Bhatt

Commonwealth

ECOTOURISM

Edition : 2026

ISBN 81-311-0063-4

Published by :

COMMONWEALTH PUBLISHERS
4831/24, Prahlad Street,
Ansari Road, Darya Ganj,
New Delhi - 110002
Ph. : 23275511, 23257835
e-mail : commonwealthbooks@gmail.com

Printed at :
Roshan Offset Printers
Delhi

PREFACE

Tourism can be defined as the act of travel for the purpose of recreation, and the provision of services for this act. It is a service industry, comprising a number of tangible and intangible components. The tangible elements include transportation systems—air, rail, road, water and now, space; hospitality services, accommodation, foods and beverages, tours, souvenirs; and related services such as banking, insurance and safety and security. The intangible elements include: rest and relaxation, culture, escape, adventure, new and different experiences.

Travel and tourism is a major industry in the world and is at the top of the league of invisible earners of foreign currency. Many sovereignties, along with their respective countries and states, depend heavily upon travel expenditures by foreigners as a source of taxation and income for the enterprises that sell services to these travellers. Consequently the development of tourism is often a strategy employed either by a non-governmental organization or a governmental agency to promote a particular region for the purpose of increasing commerce through exporting goods and services to non-locals.

During recent years the tourism industry has witnessed unprecedented growth. Increasing consumer demand for educational and participatory travel experiences has resulted in a variety of specialty niche markets such as ecotourism, cultural-heritage tourism, and agritourism. New paradigms link strategic tourism planning with sustainable development.

The leisure and tourism industry is one of the leading global economic activities, a multi-billion-dollar industry with

700 million international travellers per year around the world. Tourism is a motor for employment and income creation and, especially in poor countries, a vehicle for development. But today it is not sufficient to simply create employment without regard for the quality of jobs and the social and environmental effects of tourism in vulnerable areas. A growing number of organizations, including the tourism industry leadership, are increasingly conscious of the risks and are adopting a more responsible attitude.

The present publication provides an authoritative look at how to manage travel and tourism industry in a better way. It introduces the complexities of the tourism system so that they will be better positioned to eventually assume the managerial challenges and responsibilities in a diverse and challenging industry. The latest advancements in tourism theory and thinking, retaining the thoroughness of content, diversity of applications, regional and international issues, economic significance, tourism operators and the role of technology in the tourism industry etc. are also described elaborately. Numerous regional and global case studies and examples are included to provide an appropriately broad geographic context. This work will be highly informative and useful to students, researchers, policy makers, managers and working groups of travel and tourism industry.

B.S. Badan
Harish Bhatt

Contents

1

The Nature of Tourism

In this chapter the *Tourism System* is discussed, including definitions of tourism and associated industry elements. Considerable attention is paid to attractions as fundamental elements of the tourist experience. Both mass tourism and alternative tourism paradigms are introduced as a means by which to overview the philosophical approaches to tourism development to the present day. Finally, much of the chapter is devoted to sustainable development and sustainable tourism, including sustainable tourism indicators, for the purpose of demonstrating the relevance of this form of development to the future of the tourism industry. This discussion will provide a backdrop from which to analyse Ecotourism, which is detailed at length in Chapter 2.

Defining Tourism

As one of the world's largest industries, tourism is associated with many of the prime sectors of the world's economy. Any such phenomenon that is intricately interwoven into the fabric of life—economically, socio-culturally and environmentally—and relies on primary, secondary and tertiary levels of production and service, is difficult to define in simple terms. This difficulty is mirrored in a 1991 issue of *The Economist:*

> There is no accepted definition of what constitutes the [tourism] industry; any definition runs the risk of either overestimating or underestimating economic activity. At its simplest, the industry is one that gets people from their home to somewhere else (and back), and which provides lodging and food for them while they are away. But that does not get you

far. For example, if all the sales of restaurants were counted as travel and tourism, the figure would be artificially inflated by sales to locals. But to exclude all restaurant sales would be just as misleading.

It is this complex integration within our socio-economic system (a critical absence of focus), according to Clawson and Knetsch (1966) and Mitchell (1984), that complicates efforts to define tourism. Tourism studies are often placed poles apart in terms of philosophical approach, methodological orientation, or intent of the investigation. A variety of tourism definitions each with disciplinary attributes that reflect research initiatives corresponding to various fields. For example, tourism shares strong fundamental characteristics and theoretical foundations with the recreation and leisure studies field. According to Jansen-Verbeke and Dietvorst (1987) the terms leisure, recreation and tourism represent a type of loose, harmonious unity which focuses on the experiential and activity-based features that typify these terms. On the other hand, economic and technical/statistical definitions generally ignore the human experiential elements of the concept in favour of an approach based on the movement of people over political borders and the amount of money generated from this movement.

It is this relationship with other disciplines, e.g. psychology, sociology, anthropology, geography, economics, which seems to have defined the complexion of tourism. However, despite its strong reliance on such disciplines, some, including Leiper (1981), have advocated a move away in favour of a distinct tourism discipline. To Leiper the way in which we need to approach the tourism discipline should be built around the structure of the industry, which he considers as an open system of five elements interacting with broader environments: (1) a dynamic human element, (2) a generating region, (3) a transit region, (4) a destination region, and (5) the tourist industry. This definition is similar to one established by Mathieson and Wall (1982), who see tourism as comprising three basic elements: (1) a dynamic element, which involves travel to a selected destination; (2) a static element, which involves a stay at the destination; and (3) a consequential element, resulting from the above two, which is concerned with the effects on the economic, social and physical subsystems with which the tourist is directly or indirectly in contact. Others, including Mill and Morrison, define tourism as a system of interrelated parts. The system is 'like a spider's web—touch one part of it and reverberations will be felt throughout' (Mill and Morrison 1985: xix). Included in their tourism system are four component parts, including Market (reaching the marketplace), Travel (the purchase of travel products), Destination (the shape of travel demand), and Marketing (the selling of travel).

In recognition of the difficulty in defining tourism, Smith (1990a) feels that it is more realistic to accept the existence of a number of different definitions, each designed to serve different purposes. This may in fact prove to be the most practical of approaches to follow. In this book, tourism is defined as the interrelated system that includes tourists and the associated services that are provided and utilised (facilities, attractions, transportation and accommodation) to aid in their movement, while a tourist, as established by the World Tourism Organisation, is defined as a person travelling for pleasure for a period of at least one night, but not more than one year for international tourists and six months for persons travelling in their own countries, with the main purpose of the visit being other than to engage in activities for remuneration in the place(s) visited.

Tourism Attractions

The tourism industry includes a number of key elements that tourists rely upon to achieve their general and specific goals and needs within a destination. Broadly categorised, they include facilities, accommodation, transportation and attractions. Although an in-depth discussion of each is beyond the scope of this book, there is merit in elaborating upon the importance of tourism attractions as a fundamental element of the tourist experience. Past tourism research has tended to rely more on the understanding of attractions, and how they affect tourists, than of other components of the industry. As Gunn has suggested, 'they [attractions] represent the most important reasons for travel to destinations' (1972 : 24).

MacCannell described tourism attractions as 'empirical relationship between a tourist, a site and a marker' (1989 : 41). The tourist represents the human component, the site includes the actual destination or physical entity, and the marker represents some form of information that the tourist uses to identify and give meaning to a particular attraction. Lew (1987), however, took a different view, arguing that under the conditions of tourist-site-marker, virtually anything could become an attraction, including services and facilities. Lew chose to emphasise the objective and subjective characteristics of attractions by suggesting that researchers ought to be concerned with three main areas of the attraction :

- *Ideographic*—Describes the concrete uniqueness of a site. Sites are individually identified by name and usually associated with small regions. This is the most frequent form of attraction studied in tourism research.
- *Organisational*—The focus is not on the attractions themselves, but rather on their spatial, capacity and temporal nature. Scale continua are based on the size of the area which the attraction encompasses.
- *Cognitive*—A place that fosters the feeling of being a tourist. Attractions are places that elicit feelings related to what Relph (1976) termed 'insider' 'outsider', and the authenticity of MacCannell's (1989) front and back regions.

Leiper (1990 : 381) further added to the debate by adapting MacCannell's model into a systems definition. He wrote that:

> A tourist attraction is a systematic arrangement of three elements: a person with touristic needs, a nucleus (any feature or characteristic of a place they might visit) and at least one marker (information about the nucleus).

The type of approach established by Leiper is also reflected in the efforts of Gunn (1972), who has written at length on the importance of attractions in tourism research. Gunn produced a model of tourist attractions that contained three separate zones, including (1) the nuclei, or core of the attraction; (2) the inviolate belt, which is the space needed to set the nuclei in a context; and (3) the zone of closure, which includes desirable tourism infrastructure such as toilets and information. Gunn argued that an attraction missing one of these zones will be incomplete and difficult to manage.

Some authors, including Pearce (1982), Gunn (1988) and Leiper (1990), have made reference to the fact that attractions occur on various hierarchies of scale, from very specific and small objects within a site, to entire countries and continents. This scale variability further complicates the analysis of attractions as both sites and regions. Consequently, there exists a series of attraction cores and attraction peripheries, within different regions, between regions, and from the perspective of the types of tourists who visit them. Spatially, and with the influence of time, the number and type of attractions visited by tourists and tourist groups may create a niche; a role certain types of tourists occupy within a vacation destination. Through an analysis of space, time, and other behavioural factors, tourists can be fitted into a typology based on their utilisation and travel between selected attractions. One could make the assumption that tourist groups differ on the basis of the type of attractions they choose to visit, and according to how much time they spend at them (see Fennell 1996). The implications for the tourism industry are that often it must provide a broad range of experiences for tourists interested in different aspects of a region. A specific destination region, for example, may recognise the importance of providing a mix of touristic opportunities, from the very specific, to more general interest experiences for the tourists in search of cultural and natural experiences, in urban, rural, and back-country settings.

Attractions have also been referred to in past research as sedentary, physical entities of a cultural or natural form (Gunn 1988). Although Gunn acknowledges wildlife as a *foundation* for attractions, it has been clear that wildlife is not simply the foundation of attractions, but an attraction in and of itself. To a birder, for example, individual species become attractions of the most specific and most sought-after kind. A case in point is the annual return of a single albatross at the Hermaness National Nature Reserve in Unst, Shetland, Scotland. The arrival of this species prompts birdwatching tourists immediately to change their plans in an effort to travel to Hermaness. The albatross has become a major attraction for birder-tourists, while Hermaness, in a broader context, acts as a medium (attraction cluster) by which to present the attraction (bird). Natural attractions can be transitory in space and time, and this time may be measured for particular species in seconds, hours, days, weeks, months, seasons, or years. For tourists who travel with the prime reason to experience these transitory attractions, their movement is a source of both challenge and frustration.

Mass and Alternative Tourism : Competing Paradigms

Tourism has been both lauded and denounced for its ability to develop and therefore transform regions into completely different settings. In the former case, tourism is seen to have provided the impetus for appropriate long-term development; in the latter the ecological and sociological disturbance to transformed regions can be overwhelming. While most of the documented cases of the negative impacts of tourism are in the developing world, the developed world is certainly not an exception. Young (1983), for example, documented the transformation of a small fishing—farming community in Malta by graphically illustrating the extent to which tourism development—through an increasingly complex system of transportation, resort development and social behaviour—overwhelms such areas over time.

These days we are more prone to vilify or characterise conventional mass tourism as a beast; a monstrosity which has few redeeming qualities for the destination region, their people and their natural resource base. Consequently, mass tourism has been criticised for the fact that it dominates tourism within a region owing to its non-local orientation, and the fact that very little money spent within the destination actually stays and generates more income. It is quite often the hotel or mega-resort that is the symbol of mass tourism's domination of a region, are often created using non-local products, having little requirement for local food products, and owned by metropolitan interests. Hotel marketing occurs on the basis of high volume, attracting as many people as possible, often over seasonal periods of time. The implications of this seasonality are such that local people are at times moved in and out of paid positions that are based solely on this volume of touristic traffic. Development exists as a means by which to concentrate people in very high densities, displacing local people from traditional subsistence-style livelihoods (as outlined by Young 1983) to ones that are subservience based. Finally, the attractions that lie in and around these massive developments are created and transformed to meet the expectations and demands of visitors. Emphasis is often on commercialisation of natural and cultural resources, and the result is a contrived and inauthentic representation of, for example, a cultural theme or event that has been eroded into a distant memory.

Admittedly the picture of mass tourism painted above is outlined to illustrate the point that the tourism industry has not always operated with the interests of local people and the resource base in mind. This was most emphatically articulated through much of the tourism research that emerged in the 1980s, which argued for a new, more socially and ecologically benign alternative to mass tourism development. According to Krippendorf (1982), the philosophy behind alternative tourism (AT)—forms of tourism that advocate an approach opposite to mass conventional tourism—was to ensure that tourism policies should no longer concentrate on economic and technical necessities alone, but rather emphasise the demand for an unspoiled environment and consideration of the needs of local people. This 'softer' approach places the natural and cultural resources at the forefront of planning and development, instead of as an afterthought. Also, as an inherent function, alternative forms of tourism provide the means for countries to eliminate outside influences, and to sanction projects themselves and to participate in their development—in essence, to win back the decision-making power in essential matters rather than conceding to outside people and institutions.

AT is a generic term that encompasses a whole range of tourism strategies (e.g. 'appropriate', 'eco-', 'soft', 'responsible', 'people to people', 'controlled', 'small-scale', 'cottage' and 'green' tourism), all of which purport to offer a more benign alternative to conventional mass tourism in certain types of destinations (Conference Report 1990 cited in Weaver 1991). Dernoi (1981) illustrates that the advantages of AT will be felt in five ways—

(1) There will be benefits for the individual or family–accommodation based in local homes will channel revenue directly to families. Also families will acquire managerial skills.

(2) The local community will benefit–AT will generate direct revenue for community members, in addition to upgrading

housing standards while avoiding huge public infrastructure expenses.

(3) For the host country, AT will help avoid the leakage of tourism revenue outside the country. AT will also help prevent social tensions and may preserve local traditions.

(4) For those in the industrialised generating country, AT is ideal for cost-conscious travellers or for people who prefer close contacts with locals.

(5) There will be benefits for international relations–AT may promote international-inter-regional-intercultural understanding.

More specifically, Weaver (1993) has analysed the potential benefits of an AT design from the perspective of accommodation, attractions, market, economic impact and regulation (Table 1.1). This more sensitive approach to tourism development strives to satisfy the needs of local people, tourists, and the resource base in a complementary rather than a competitive manner.

Some researchers, however, are quick to point out that as an option to mass tourism, full-fledged alternative tourism cannot replace conventional tourism simply because of mass tourism's varied and many-sided associated phenomena (Cohen 1987). Instead, it is more realistic to concentrate efforts in attempts to reform the worst prevailing situations, not the development of alternatives. Butler (1990) feels that mass tourism has not been rejected outright for two main reasons. The first is economic, in that it provides a significant amount of foreign exchange for countries; the second is socio-psychological and relates to the fact that—

> many people seem to enjoy being a mass tourist. They actually like not having to make their own travel arrangements, not having to find accommodation when they arrive at a destination, being able to obtain goods and services without learning a foreign language, being able to stay in reasonable, in some cases considerable comfort, being able to eat reasonably familiar food, and not having to spend vast amounts of money or time to achieve these goals.
>
> (Butler 1990: 40)

Table 1.1
Potential Benefits Derived from an Alternative Tourism Strategy

Accommodation

- Does not overwhelm the community.
- Benefits (jobs, expenditures) are more evenly distributed.
- Less competition with homes and businesses for the use of infrastructure.
- A larger percentage of revenues accrue to local areas.
- Greater opportunity for local entrepreneurs to participate in the tourism sector.

Attractions

- Authenticity and uniqueness of community is promoted and enhanced.
- Attractions are educational and promote self-fulfilment.
- Locals can benefit from existence of the attractions even if tourists are not present.

Market

- Tourists do not overwhelm locals in numbers; stress is avoided.
- 'Drought/deluge' cycles are avoided, and equilibrium is fostered.
- A more desirable visitor type.
- Less vulnerability to disruption within a single major market.

Economic Impact

- Economic diversity is promoted to avoid single-sector dependence.
- Sectors interact and reinforce each other.
- Net revenues are proportionally higher; money circulates within the community.
- More jobs and economic activity are generated.

Regulation

- Community makes the critical development/strategy decisions.
- Planning to meet ecological, social and economic carrying capacities.
- Holistic approach stresses integration and well-being of community interests.
- Long-term approach takes into account the welfare of future generations.
- Integrity of foundation assets is protected.
- Possibility of irreversibilities is reduced.

Sustainable Development and Tourism

The measurement of development (i.e. a nation's stage of socio-economic advancement) has conventionally been accomplished through the implementation of a number of key economic indicators. Among others, these include variables such as protein intake, access to potable water, air quality, fuel, health care, education, employment, GDP and GNP. The so-called 'developed' world (countries like Australia, the USA, Canada, and those of Western Europe) therefore is defined by the existence of these socio-economic conditions, whereby those with more are considered more highly developed. Furthermore, one's level of development, either objectively or subjectively, is often equated or synonymous with one's perceived stage of 'civilisation', whereby progress (usually economic) is a key to the relationship between who is civilised and who is not. The *Oxford English Dictionary* defines civilisation as an 'advanced stage of social development', and civilise as 'bring out of barbarism, enlighten'. The point to be made is that perhaps our perception of what is developed and what isn't, what is civilised and what isn't, is a matter of debate and one that our more recent approaches to development need to better address. For example, it has been noted that the most developed 20 per cent of the world's population (those in the 'West') are thought to use some 80 per cent of the world's resources with which to achieve development. If it is our goal to have the entire world 'developed' according to this Western paradigm, the planet will be in serious jeopardy. Perhaps in a hundred or two hundred years *Homo sapiens* will look back at Western civilisation as the most barbaric time period in recorded history.

Deming (1996) shares the view that humanity needs to take a good long look at civilisation. She writes that people have an insatiable hunger to see more and more of the planet, and to get closer and closer to its natural attractions. This behaviour surfaces continually in tourism as the tentacles of the tourist seek to push the fine line that exists between acceptable and unacceptable human-wildlife interactions. For example, animal harassment regularly occurs in Point Pelee National Park in Ontario, Canada, as thousands of birders converge on the spring migration of birds in the park. Despite posted warnings, tourists continue to venture off the designated paths in identifying and photographing species. Deming asks: in the face of global warming, diminishing habitat, and massive extinctions, what can it mean to be civilised? Her response is a plead for limits, both social and ecological, in facing the enemy within :

> As Pogo said during the Vietnam War, 'We've seen the enemy and it is us'. Suddenly we are both the invading barbarians and the only ones around to protect the city. Each one of us is at the center of the civilised world and on its edge.
>
> (Deming 1996 :32)

Milgrath (1989) talked of values as fundamental to everything we do (see also Forman 1990). He argues that humans have as a central value their personal desire to preserve their lives. This naturally evolves into a concern and value for other people—a social value. Milgrath suggests that it is inappropriate to elevate the preservation of each human life to a central concern because every person dies and this social preservation can never be realised. He feels instead that we should value the preservation of our ecosystems over society. Beyond the socially oriented values of society, Milgrath says we have given top priority to economic development, the result being that society will not be able to sustain itself over the long-term.

Sustainable development has been proposed as a model that can have utility in creating the impetus for structural change within society, one that ventures away from a strictly socio-economic focus to one where development 'meets the goals of the present without compromising the ability of future generations to meet their own needs' (World Commission on Environment and Development 1987 : 43). As such, the principles of ecology are essential to the process of economic development (Redcliff 1987), with the aim of increasing the material standards of people living in the world who are impoverished (Barbier 1987). Even more fundamentally, though, it would seem more inspiring to hope that sustainable development would increase the moral standards of people living everywhere, which might naturally spill over into the realm of economics, which we know is critical to our viability. Tourism's international importance as an engine for economic growth, as well as its potential for growth, makes it particularly relevant to sustainable development. Consequently there is a wealth of literature emerging that is directly related to the sustainability of tourism, however broadly defined.

One of the first action strategies on tourism and sustainability emerged from the Globe '90 conference in British Columbia, Canada. Here, representatives from the tourism industry, government, non-governmental organisations (NGOs), and academia discussed the importance of the environment in sustaining the tourism industry, and how poorly planned tourism developments often erode the very qualities of the natural and human environment that attract visitors. The conference delegates suggested that the goals of sustainable tourism are: (1) to develop greater awareness and understanding of the significant contributions that tourism can make to environment and the economy; (2) to promote equity and development; (3) to improve the quality of life of the host community; (4) to provide a high quality of experience for the visitor; and (5) to maintain the quality of the environment on which the foregoing objectives depend. Although their definition of sustainable tourism development was somewhat non-committal (i.e. 'meeting the needs of present tourist and host region while protecting and enhancing opportunity for the future'), a number of good recommendations were developed for policy, government, NGOs, the tourism industry, tourists and international organisations. For example, the policy section contains 15 recommendations related to how tourism should be promoted, developed, defined, in addition to a series of regional, interregional, and spatial and temporal implications. One of the policy recommendations states that 'sustainable tourism requires the placing of guidelines for levels and types of acceptable growth but does not preclude new facilities and experiences' (Globe '90 1990 : 6).

From the perspective of financial prosperity and growth, there is an economic rationale for sustainability; as McCool (1995 : 3) asserts, 'once communities lose the character that makes them distinctive and attractive to nonresidents, they have lost their ability to vie for tourist-based income in an increasingly global and competitive marketplace'. In addition, McCool quotes Fallon is suggesting that sustainability is all about the pursuit of goals and measuring progress towards them. No longer is it appropriate to gauge appropriate development by physical output or economic bottom lines; these must also be consideration of social order and justice (see also Hall 1992 and Urry 1992). McCool feels, therefore, that in order for sustainable tourism to be successful, humans must consider the following: (1) how tourists value and use natural environments; (2) how communities are enhanced through tourism; (3) identification of tourism's social and ecological impacts; and (4) management of these impacts.

Accordingly, many researchers and associations have initiated the process of determining and measuring impacts. As outlined above, Globe '90 was one of the initial and integral forces in linking tourism with sustainable development. This was followed by Globe '92 (Hawkes and Williams 1993) and the move from principles to practice in implementing measures of sustainability in tourism. Even so, it was recognised in this conference that there was much work to be done in implementing sustainable principles in tourism, as emphasised by Roy (in Sadler 1992 : ix) :

> Sustainable tourism is an extension of the new emphasis on sustainable development. Both remain concepts. I have not found a single example of either in India. The closest for tourism is in Bhutan. Very severe control of visitors—2000 per year—conserves the environment and the country's unique socio-cultural identity. Even there, trekking in the high altitudes, I find the routes littered with the garbage of civilisation.

Although many examples exist in the literature on tourism and sustainable development (see Nelson *et al.* 1993), few sustainable tourism projects have withstood the test of time. An initiative that has received some exposure in the literature is the Bali Sustainable Development Project, coordinated through the University of Waterloo, Canada, and Gadjahmada University in Indonesia (see Wall 1993 and Mitchell 1994). This is a project that has been applied at a multisectoral level. Tourism, then, is one of many sectors, albeit a prime one, that drives the Balinese economy. Wall (1993) suggests that some of the main conclusions from his work on the project are as follows—

(1) Be as culturally sensitive as possible in developing a sustainable development strategy.

(2) Work within existing institutional frameworks as opposed to creating new ones.

(3) Multi-sectoral planning is critical to a sustainable development strategy and means must be created to allow all affected stakeholders to participate in decision-making.

(See also the work of Cooper (1995) on the offshore islands of the UK and the work of Aylward *et al.* (1996) on the sustainability of the Monteverde Cloud Forest Preserve in Costa Rica as good examples of tourism and sustainability.) The integration of tourism with other land uses in a region has also been addressed by Butler (1993 : 221), who sees integration as 'the incorporation of an activity into an area on a basis acceptable to other activities and the environment within the general goal of sustainable or long-term development'. Butler identified complementarity, compatibility and competitiveness as variables that could be used as a first step in prioritising land uses, where complementarity leads to a higher degree of integration and competitiveness leads to segregation of the activity relative to other land uses.

Other models have been more unisectoral in their approach to the pace of tourism within a destination region. These have tended to identify a range of indicators that identify a sustainable approach or unsustainable approach to the delivery of tourism. Examples include Canova's (1994) illustration of how tourists can be responsible towards the environment and local populations; Forsyth's (1995) overview of sustainable tourism and self-regulation; Moscardo *et al.*s' (1996) look at ecologically sustainable forms of tourism accommodation; and Consulting and Audit Canada's (1995) guide to the development of core and site-specific sustainable tourism indicators (see also Manning 1996). Table 1.2 identifies the core indicators identified in this document. These core indicators (e.g. site protection, stress, use intensity, waste management, and so on) must, according to the report, be used in concert with specific site or destination indicators. This report identifies two categories of this latter group of indicators: (1) supplementary ecosystem-specific indicators (applied to specific biophysical land and water regions), and (2) site-specific indicators, which are developed for a particular site. Table 1.3

Table 1.2
Core Indicators of Sustainable Tourism

Indicator	*Specific measures*
Site protection	Category of site protection according to IUCN index
Stress	Tourist numbers visiting site (per annum/peak month)
Use intensity	Intensity of use in peak period (persons/hectare)
Social impact	Ratio of tourists to locals (peak period and over time)
Development control	Existence of environmental review procedure or formal controls over development of site and use densities
Waste management	Percentage of sewage from site receiving treatment (additional indicators may include structural limits of other infrastructural capacity on site, such as water supply)
Planning process	Existence of organised regional plan for tourist destination region (including tourism component)
Critical ecosystems	Number of rare or endangered species
Consumer satisfaction	Level of satisfaction by visitors (survey-based)
Local satisfaction	Level of satisfaction by visitors (survey-based)
Tourism contribution to local economy	Proportion of total economic activity generated by tourism
Composite indices	
Carrying capacity	Composite early warning measure of key factors affecting the ability of the site to support different levels of tourism.
Site stress	Composite measure of levels of impact on the site (its natural/cultural attributes due to tourism and other sector cumulative stress)
Attractivity	Qualitative measure of those site attributes that make it attractive to tourism and can change over time

Source : Consulting and Audit Canada (1995)

Table 1.3
Ecosystem-specific Indicators

Ecosystem	*Sample indicators*[a]
Coastal zones	Degradation (percentage of beach degraded, eroded) Use intensity (persons per metre of accessible beach) Water quality (faecal coliform and heavy metals counts)
Mountain regions	Erosion (percentage of surface area eroded) Biodiversity (key species counts) Access to key sites (hours' wait)
Managed wildlife parks	Species health (reproductive success, species diversity) Use intensity (ratio of visitors to game) Encroachment (percentage of park affected by unauthorised activity)
Ecologically unique sites	Ecosystem degradation (number and mix of species, percentage area with change in cover) Stress on site (number of operators (using site) Number of tourist sitings of key species (percentage success)
Urban environments	Safety (crime numbers) Waste counts (amounts of rubbish, costs) Pollution (air pollution counts)
Cultural sites (built)	Site degradation (restoration/repair costs) Structure degradation (precipitation acidity, air pollution counts) Safety (crime levels)
Cultural sites (traditional)	Potential social stress (ratio average income of tourists/locals) In season sites (percentage of vendors open year round) Antagonism (reported incidents between locals and tourists)
Small islands	Currency leakage (percentage of loss from total tourism revenues) Ownership (percentage foreign ownership of tourism establishments) Water availability (costs, remaining supply)

Source : Manning 1996.

Note : (a)—These ecosystem-specific indicators are merely suggested, and act as supplements to core indicators.

provides an overview of some of these 'secondary' ecosystem indicators.

Some publications have discussed tourism and sustainability from the perspective of codes of ethics. While indicators are variables that are identified and used to measure and monitor tourism impacts, codes of ethics or conduct are lists designed to elicit a change in behaviour of particular stakeholder groups; a form of compliance for acceptable behaviour at a tourism setting. The *Beyond the Green Horizon* paper on sustainable tourism (Tourism Concern 1992) is a good example of this form of education. To Tourism Concern, sustainable tourism is :

> tourism and associated infrastructures that, both now and in the future: operate within natural capacities for the regeneration and future productivity of natural resources; recognise the contribution that people and communities, customs and lifestyles, make to the tourism experience; accept that these people must have an equitable share in the economic benefits of tourism; are guided by the wishes of local people and communities in the host areas.

Nothing is measured but 'rules' are stated for the purpose of prompting or reinforcing this appropriate behaviour. A further elaboration of Tourism Concern's ten guiding principles can be found in Figure 1.1.

The Tourism Industry Association of Canada (1995) joined forces with the National Round Table on the Environment and the Economy in creating a document that demonstrates commitment and responsibility to protecting the environment through cooperation with other sectors and governments at all levels. Their sustainable tourism guidelines were developed for tourists, the tourism industry, industry associations, accommodation, food services tour, operators, and Ministries of Tourism. Each of these sections contains appropriate guidelines that deal with policy and planning; the tourism experience; the host community; development; natural, cultural, and historic resources; conservation of natural resources; environmental protection; marketing; research and education; public awareness; industry cooperation; and the global village.

① Using Resources Sustainably

The conservation and sustainable use of resources—natural, social and cultural—is crucial and makes long-term business sense.

② Reducing Over-consumption and Waste

Reduction of over-consumption and waste avoids the costs of restoring long-term environmental damage and contributes to the quality of tourism.

③ Maintaining Diversity

Maintaining and promoting natural, social and cultural diversity is essential for long-term sustainable tourism, and creates a resilient base for the industry.

④ Integrating Tourism into Planning

Tourism development which is integrated into a national and local strategic planning framework, and which undertakes EIAs, increases the long-term viability of tourism.

⑤ Supporting Local Economies

Tourism that supports a wide range of local economic activities, and which takes environmental costs/values into account, both protects those economies and avoids environmental damage.

⑥ Involving Local Communities

The full involvement of local communities in the tourism sector not only benefits them and the environment in general but also improves the quality of the tourism experience.

⑦ Consulting Stakeholders and the Public

Consultation between the tourism industry and local communities, organisations and institutions is essential if they are to work alongside each other and resolve potential conflicts of interest.

⑧ Training Staff

Staff training which integrates sustainable tourism into work practices, along with recruitment of local personnel at all levels, improves the quality of the tourism product.

⑨ Marketing Tourism Responsibly

Marketing that provides tourists with full and responsible information increases respect for the natural, social and cultural environments of destination areas and enhances customer satisfaction.

⑩ Undertaking Research

Ongoing research and monitoring by the industry using effective data collection and analysis is essential in solving problems and bringing benefits to destinations, the industry and consumers.

Fig. 1.1 : Principles for sustainable tourism.

Source : Tourism Concern, 1992.

A final publication that merits attention in this section is the work of the Federation of Nature and National Parks of Europe (1993). Its comprehensive look at sustainable tourism in Europe's nature and national parks provides good insight into the challenge of implementing sustainability in that part of the world. Many of the protected areas in Europe are situated in rural working landscapes (e.g. England, Wales, Luxembourg) and must contend with different pressures as compared with some of the larger and less densely populated areas surrounding the protected areas of Australia and New Zealand, Canada and the United States. However, Europe also contains many large national parks and biosphere reserves that are maintained accordingly. In both cases (rural and wilderness environments) policy-makers and practitioners are charged with the task of implementing sustainable tourism in these varied settings. The European national parks document recognises that people must be able to improve the quality of their lives, maintain jobs, improve their economy, enjoy their cultures, and promote harmony between cultures. These must be accomplished with an eye to environmental education, political support for the environment, and the protection of heritage values through restorative projects and direct practical help.

Sustainable tourism, however, is not without its critics. Hunter (1995), for example, suggests that the current approach to sustainable tourism development is one that is flawed because it condones the planning and management of tourism in a manner inconsistent with the design of sustainable development. In particular, tourism does not adequately address issues of geographical scale and intersectoral cooperation which are so important to achieving sustainable development. Furthermore, Macbeth (1994) calls attention to the fact that sustainable tourism is more reactionary than proactive in nature. Macbeth suggests that 'the history of capitalism is full of examples of how reactionary tendencies are easily co-opted by capitalism to sustain its own existence, thus extending the *status quo* of exploitive relations rather than overthrowing them' (*ibid.*: 44). This will continue to occur, according to Macbeth, unless the present form of capitalism is overcome.

CASE STUDY 1.1

Sustainable Tourism and the Green Villages of Austria

Understanding the vital link between landscape and tourism, Austria has embarked upon a policy of sustainable tourism with the aim of preservation and an overall improvement in the quality of the natural environment. Specifically, the following measures have been proposed:

(1) A straightening out of the demand curve to avoid peak demands and burdens;

(2) reducing the consumption of space for tourism;

(3) preservation of natural landscapes;

(4) cooperation with other industries, in particular agriculture and forestry;

(5) professionalism within the industry; and

(6) a changing of the behaviour of tourists.

One of the most significant programmes in Austria is the Green Village endeavour, which is designed to allow communities to accommodate the growing demands of tourism in a sustainable way. Towns are encouraged to incorporate solar panels in their heating, restrict building height to no more than three storeys, keep parking places a minimum of 80 metres away from buildings to eliminate noise and fumes, keep motorways at least 3 km away from Green Villages, restrict vehicular traffic through villages, designate cycle paths, recycle, restrict building to the town site only, eliminate single-crop farming in adjacent farmlands, discriminate in favour of sustainable craftsmen, build hotels using natural products, insist that farmers be able to sell their products locally, and use local, natural pharmaceuticals. Such a philosophy, it is thought, will benefit both communities and the tourism industry.

McKercher (1993a) feels that tourism is vulnerable to losing sustainability for four main reasons. First, tourism is not recognised as a natural resource-dependent industry; second, the tourism industry is invisible, especially in urban areas; third, tourism is electorally weak, with little support in government; and fourth, there is a distinct lack of leadership driving the industry, which ultimately makes tourism vulnerable to attacks from other land users. McKercher cites the example of resource use in northern Ontario as a case in point. In this region the economy has been dominated politically by the large extractive industries (forestry and mining). The disaggregated structure of the tourism industry in Ontario's north (predominantly outfitters and lodges) prevents it from having any political decision-making influence at all.

Other critical reviews of tourism and sustainability include Goodall and Cater's (1996) belief that sustainable tourism will probably not be achieved, despite the most committed environmental performance, and Burr's (1995) work illustrating that sustainable tourism development is unlikely to occur unless the people of rural tourism communities work together to make it happen. There appears to be certain agreement that if sustainability is to occur at all, it must be done at the local level, and perhaps shaped loosely by a broader national or international policy. The notions of policy and local participation have been examined by Laarman and Gregersen (1994), who feel that sustainable nature tourism policy must include the following three areas: (1) national support and advanced planning, (2) appropriate pricing and revenue policies; and (3) local participation and benefits.

Some authors have identified unique sustainable tourism market segments, suggesting that each uses the natural environment, has long-term economic benefits, involves continuous environmental protection ,and stimulates local community development. Although each of the foregoing variables can be used to define sustainable tourism, it is important to realise that AT may be no more sustainable than Cancun and the nearby Cozumel Island if improperly managed, and there are decidedly few examples proven to be properly managed. It is, therefore, potentially dangerous to look at sustainable tourism as a specific market, instead of from site-specific or regional case studies.

Figure 1.2 illustrates that sustainability has to be more than simply one aspect of the industry (e.g. accommodation) working in a sustainable way. The illustration recognises that in essence the tourism industry experiences a tremendous degree of fragmentation by virtue of the fact that consistency in sustainability is not likely to be found across all sectors. The aim, then, for sustainability is to ensure that all aspects of the industry are working in concert. In addition, the figure incorporates the notion of both human and physical elements working within each of the four sectors; that is, the fact that the people working at a physical attraction very much dictate the extent to which sustainability is achieved at the site.

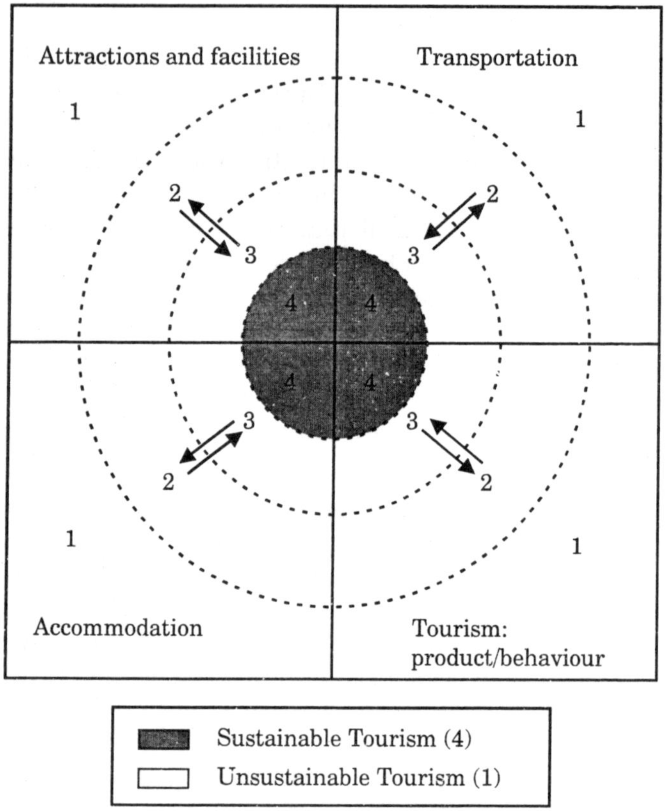

Fig. 1.2 : Degrees of Sustainable Tourism.

Conceptualising Tourism and Sustainability

In the previous discussion, mass tourism, AT, and sustainable tourism have been analysed individually. The relationship that they share, however, can be more fully appreciated in the conceptual framework shown in Figure 1.3. In a general sense, the illustration provides a good sense of the relative size of mass tourism and alternative tourism according to the corresponding circles in the diagram. Although mass tourism may be said to be predominantly unsustainable, more recently new and existing developments in the industry have attempted to encourage more sustainable practice through various measures, some of which include the controlled use of electricity, a rotating laundry schedule, and the disposal of wastes (the arrow indicates that there is a move towards an increasing degree of sustainability in this sector). On the other hand, the illustration indicates that most forms of alternative tourism are sustainable in nature (in theory). The AT sphere is shown to comprise two types of tourism, socio cultural tourism and Ecotourism. Socio-cultural AT includes, for example, rural or farm tourism, where a large portion of the touristic experience is founded upon the cultural milieu that corresponds to the environment in which farms operate. Ecotourism, however, involves a type of tourism that is less socio-cultural in its orientation, and more dependent upon nature and natural resources as the primary component or motivator of the trip, hence the division within the AT sphere (see Chapter 2 for

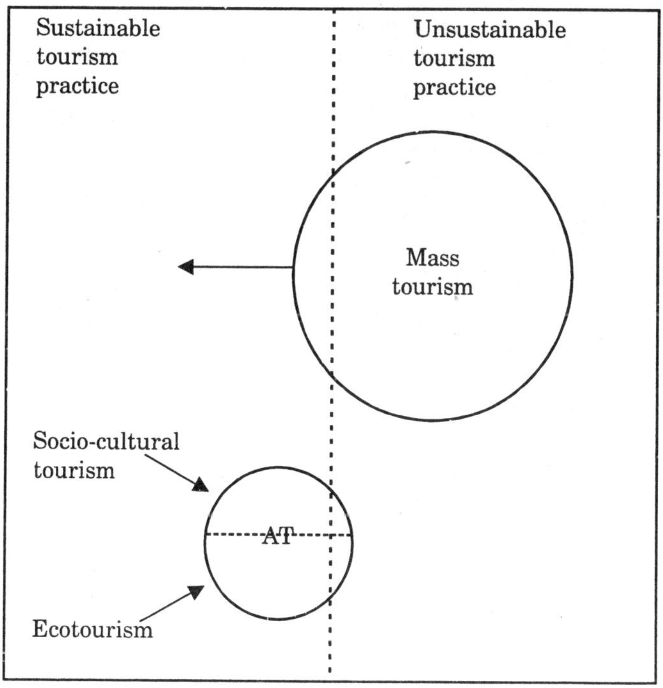

Fig. 1.3. : Tourism relationships.

an extensive overview of Ecotourism definitions and research). The focus of this book is on this lower half of the AT circle only, and the belief that Ecotourism is distinct from mass tourism and various other forms of AT.

CONCLUSION

Given the emergent wealth of literature on tourism, AT and sustainability, one cannot help but reflect on where we have been, but also on what is missing. Researchers have written countless reports, codes of conduct, guidelines, and indicators, but few attempts and successes can be drawn upon to point the direction, as illustrated in Butler's (1991) sobering analysis of tourism, environment and sustainable development. Perhaps it is still too early, and these anticipated successes will be the next stage of tourism's rather tenuous relationship with sustainability. However, there is a pressing need to move beyond the rhetoric; beyond the table and into practice, for according to Leslie (1994 : 35), 'tourism in terms of practice in developing countries is a mirror in which we see the possible mistakes identifiable retrospectively in the development and wasteful consumerist lifestyles of the west'. One cannot discount the importance of the public in operationalising AT and sustainable tourism practices. People have the power to demand goods and services that are developed and presented in an ecologically friendly manner. The public must demand accountability of tourism products, and tourism service providers must demonstrate an adherence to an appropriate vision in striving for meritorious achievements in the area of sustainable development. In doing so, it is those who achieve such lofty levels who may ultimately prosper financially.

2

Ecotourism and Ecotourists

As an extension or outgrowth of alternative tourism (AT), Ecotourism has grown as a consequence of the dissatisfaction with conventional forms of tourism which have, in a general sense, ignored social and ecological elements of foreign regions in favour of a more anthropocentric and strictly profit centred approach to the delivery of tourism products. This chapter presents an in-depth analysis of ecotourism from the perspective of history, definition, and linkages to other related forms of tourism (i.e. adventure tourism and cultural tourism). A brief discussion of tourism typologies is offered as a means by which to understand better the documented differences that exist between ecotourists and other types of travellers.

Ecotourism

Until recently, there has been some confusion surrounding the etymology or origin of the term 'ecotourism', as evident in the tremendous volume of literature on the topic. For example, Orams (1995) and Hvenegaard (1994) write that the term can be traced back only to the late 1980s, while others (Higgins 1996) suggest that it can be traced to the late 1970s, through the work of Miller (see Miller 1989) on eco-development. One of the consistent themes emergent in the literature supports the fact that Ceballos-Lascuráin was the first to coin the phrase in the early 1980s (see Thompson 1995). He defined it as 'travelling to relatively undisturbed or uncontaminated natural areas with the specific objective of studying, admiring and enjoying the scenery and its wild plants and animals, as well as any existing cultural manifestations (both past and present) found in these areas'

(Boo 1990 : xiv). In an interview (van der Merwe 1996), Ceballos-Lascuráin illustrates that his initial reference to the phrase occurred in 1983, while he was in the process of developing PRONATURA, an NGO in Mexico. Recently, however, the term has been traced further back to the work of Hetzer (1965), who used it to explain the intricate relationship between tourists and the environments and cultures in which they inter act. Hetzer identified four fundamental pillars that needed to be followed for a more responsible form of tourism. These included: (1) minimum environmental impact; (2) minimum impact on—and maximum respect for—host cultures; (3) maximum economic benefits to the host country's grassroots; and (4) maximum recreational' satisfaction to participating tourists. The development of the concept of ecotourism grew, according to Hetzer (personal communication, October 1997), as a culmination of dissatisfaction with governments' and society's negative approach to development, especially from an ecological point of view. Nelson (1994) also adopts this particular stand in illustrating that the idea of Ecotourism is in fact an old one, which manifested itself during the late 1960s and early 1970s, when researchers became concerned over inappropriate use of natural resources. Nelson suggests that the term 'eco-development' was introduced as a means by which to reduce such development.

In other related research, Fennell (1998) found evidence of Canadian government 'ecotours' which were operational during the mid-1970s. These ecotours centred around the Trans-Canada Highway and were developed on the basis of different ecological zones found along the course of the highway. The first of these encounters was developed in 1976. Based on the ecozone concept, they were felt to be rather progressive for the time despite the lack of a focused look at low impact, sustainability, community development, and the moral philosophy labels that are attached to ecotourism in the 1990s. The ecotours were developed at a time when the Canadian government felt in important to allow Canadian and foreign travellers to appreciate the human-land relationship in Canada, through the interpretation of the natural environment. Although a set definition of ecotourism was not provided, each of the ecotour guides contains the following foreword :

> Ecotours are prepared by the Canadian Forestry Service to help you, as a traveller, understand the features of the landscape you see as you cross the country. Both natural and human history are described and interpreted. The route covered by the Ecotours is divided into major landscape types, or Ecozones, and a map of each Ecozone shows the location of interesting features (identified by code numbers). While most features can be seen from your car, stops are suggested for some of them. Distances between points of interest are given in kilometres. Where side trips are described, distances are given to the turnoff from the highway. You will derive the maximum value from this Ecotour if you keep a record of the distance travelled and read the information on each point of interest before reaching it. (Fennell 1998 : 232)

Fennell goes on to suggest that ecotourism most likely has a convergent evolution, 'where many places and people independently responded to the need for more nature travel opportunities in line with society's efforts to become more ecologically minded' (Fennell 1998 : 234), as also suggested by Nelson (see above). This evidence comes at a time when researchers have been struggling to find common ground between ecotourism and its relationship to other forms of tourism, related and unrelated. (For other early references on ecotourism see Mathieson and Wall 1982; and Romeril 1985).

There seems to be universal acceptance of the fact that Ecotourism was viable long before the 1980s in practice, if not in name. For example, Blangy and Nielson (1993) illustrate that the travel department of the American Museum of Natural History has conducted natural history tours since 1953. Probably the finest examples of the evolution of ecotourism can be found in the African wildlife-based examples of tourism developed in the early twentieth century and, to some, the nature tourism enterprises of the mid-nineteenth century (Wilson 1992). There are examples in the literature that illustrate that human beings, at least since the Romantic period, have travelled to wilderness for the intrinsic nature of the experience. Nash writes that during the nineteenth century many people travelled both in Europe and North America for the primary purpose of enjoying the outdoors, as illustrated in the following passage :

> Alexis de Tocqeville resolved to see wilderness during his 1831 trip to the United States, and in Michigan Territory in July the young Frenchman found himself at last on the fringe of civilisation. But when he informed the frontiersmen of his desire to travel for pleasure into the primitive forest, they thought him mad. The Americans required considerable persuasion from Tocqueville to convince them that his interests lay in matters other than lumbering or land speculation.
>
> (Nash 1982 : 23)

Tocqueville was after something that we consider as an essential psychological factor in travel: novelty. Nash (1982) credits the intellectual revolution in the eighteenth and nineteenth centuries as the push needed to inspire the belief that unmodified nature could act as a deep spiritual and psychological tonic. It required the emergence of a group of affluent and cultured persons who largely resided in urban environments to garnish this appreciation (e.g. Jean-Jacques Rousseau and John Ruskin). For these people, Nash (*ibid.*: 347) writes, 'wilderness could become an intriguing novelty and even a deep spiritual and psychological need'. In the United States, the sentiment at the time was not as strong as it was in Europe, where 'as late as the 1870s almost all nature tourists on the American frontier continued to be foreigners' (*ibid.*: 348).

When Americans did start travelling to the wild parts of their country it was the privileged classes that held the exclusive rights. A trip to Yellowstone in the 1880s, according to O'Gara (1996), was about three times as expensive as travel to Europe at the time. There was no question that those from the city were especially taken with Yellowstone's majesty, but their mannerisms left much to be desired, as evident in an account of such tourists by Rudyard Kipling (*ibid.*: 56) :

> It is not the ghastly vulgarity, the oozing, rampant Bessemer steel self-sufficiency and ignorance of the men that revolts me, so much as the display of these same qualities in the womenfolk. . . . All the young ladies. . . remarked that [Old Faithful] was 'elegant' and betook themselves to writing their names in the bottoms of the shallow pools. Nature fixes the insult indelibly, and the after-years will learn that 'Hattie,' 'Sadie,' 'Mamie,' 'Sophie,' and so forth, have taken out their hairpins and scrawled in the face of Old Faithful.

Concepts and Variables: Definitions of Ecotourism

Given the ambiguity associated with the historical origins of ecotourism, the purpose of the present section is to identify the key features, concepts, and principles of the term, especially the link between nature tourism, (or nature-oriented tourism) and Ecotourism. For example, Laarman and Durst, in their early reference to ecotourism, defined it as a nature tourism in which the 'traveller is drawn to a destination because of his or her interest in one or more features of that destination's natural history. The visit combines education, recreation, and often adventure' (Laarman and Durst 1987 : 5). In addition, these authors were perhaps the first to make reference to nature tourism's hard and soft dimensions, based on the physical rigour of the experience and also the level of interest in natural history (Figure 2.1). Laarman and Durst suggested that scientists would in most likelihood be more dedicated than casual in their pursuit of ecotourism, and that some types of ecotourists would be more willing to endure hardships than others in order to secure their experiences. The letter 'B' in Figure 2.1 identifies a harder ecotourism experience based on a more difficult or rigorous experience, and also based on the dedication shown by the ecotourist relative to the interest in the activity.

A subsequent definition by these authors (Laarman and Durst 1993) identifies a conceptual difference between ecotourism and nature tourism. In recognising the difficulties in defining nature tourism, they establish both a narrow and broad scope to its definition. Narrowly, they say, it refers to operators running nature-oriented tours; however, broadly it applies to tourism's use of natural resources including beaches and country landscapes. In their research they define nature tourism as 'tourism focused principally on natural resources such as relatively undisturbed parks and natural areas, wetlands, wildlife reserves, and other areas of protected flora, fauna, and habitats' (*ibid.*: 2). Given this perspective, there appears to be some consensus mounting in the literature that describes ecotourism as one part of a broader nature-based tourism. This becomes evident in the discussion by Goodwin (1996 : 287), who wrote that *nature tourism*

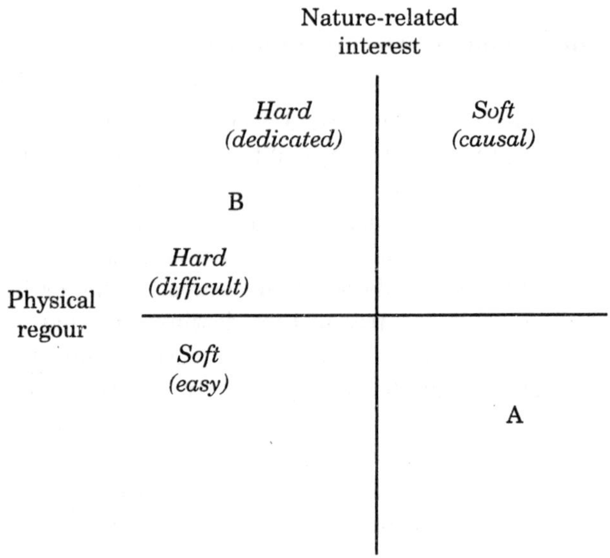

Fig. 2.1 : Hard and Soft Dimensions of Ecotourism.

> encompasses all forms of tourism—mass tourism, adventure tourism, low-impact tourism, ecotourism—which use natural resources in a wild or undeveloped form—including species, habitat, landscape, scenery and salt and fresh-water features. Nature tourism is travel for the purpose of enjoying undeveloped natural areas or wildlife.

And conversely, that *ecotourism* is

> low impact nature tourism which contributes to the maintenance of species and habitats either directly through a contribution to conservation and/or indirectly by providing revenue to the local community sufficient for local people to value, and therefore protect, their wildlife heritage area as a source of income.
>
> (Goodwin 1996 : 288)

Apart from the differences apparent in the work of Goodwin, some of the key variables or principles that separate ecotourism from its more broad-based nature counterpart include an educative component and a sustainability component (Blamey 1995), and the ethical nature of the experience, (Kutay 1989; Wight 1993a; Hawkes and Williams 1993; Wallace and Pierce 1996).

In view of the relationship between the two concepts, there does seem to be some merit in linking ecotourism to nature tourism, given the tremendous variety of nature-related tourism interests. However, there is also ambiguity in separating nature tourism from other forms of tourism, all of which rely upon the use of natural resources. Even mass, resort-based tourism relies upon undeveloped resources (i.e. beaches and the ocean) as a central component of the product and experience. An important aspect of Goodwin's discussion includes the fact that not all types of nature tourism are necessarily compatible with each other or the environment. Examples include hunting and birdwatching, which place different demands on the resource base, and users, and which have a different managerial focus (if managed at all) which is based on the consumptive nature of these activities. The importance of management in guiding the ecotourism product was central to the work of Fennell and Eagles (1990), who included the resource tour as the principal component of the ecotourism experience; the service industry, including tour operation, government policy, resource management, and community

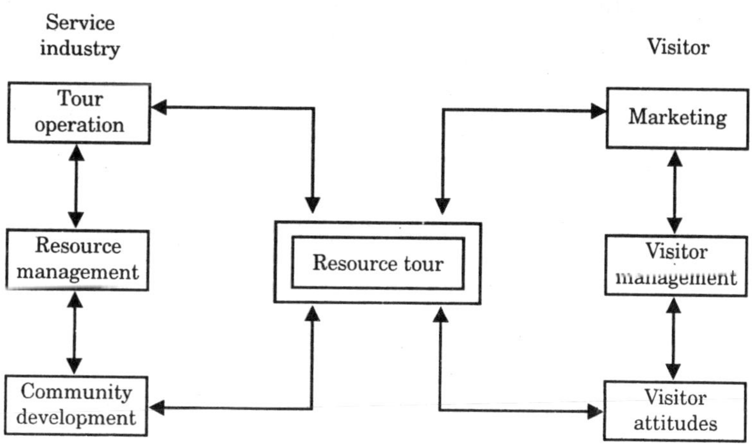

Fig. 2.2 : Ecotourism framework.

development; and the visitor experience, based on marketing, visitor management, and visitor attitudes (Figure 2.2). In their work, Fennell and Eagles recognised the value in management from the visitors' perspective, but also from the community and resource- based perspectives (see also Hvenegaard 1994 for a good description of ecotourism conceptual frameworks).

CASE STUDY 2.1

Nature Tourism in Texas

Ecotourism in Texas provides an excellent example of how ecotourism is subsumed by nature tourism. In Texas, nature tourism is defined as 'discretionary travel to natural areas that conserves the environmental, social and cultural values while generating an economic benefit to the local community' (Texas Parks and Wildlife 1996 : 2). Although hunting and fishing are reported to be traditional mainstays of nature tourism in Texas, the Task Force on Nature Tourism states that non-consumptive activities such as bird and wildlife watching, nature study and photography, biking, camping, rafting and hiking have experienced the greatest growth over the past few years. In Texas, the task force reports that tourism is the third largest industry in Texas, generating $ 23 billion annually, with the potential to replace oil and gas, and manufacturing as the highest income earner by the turn of the century.

The Great Texas Coastal Birding Trail is a key Ecotourism attraction in the Lone Star State. The goal of this trail is to increase the opportunities for nature tourism in the coastal communities of Texas, in addition to conveying the value of conservation to people living in the region. Although the trail was conceived by the Texas Parks and Wildlife Department, it was made possible by transportation enhancement funds and the Texas Department of Transportation. The trail utilises existing transportation infrastructure (viewing platforms and boardwalks are being added on a continual basis) in creating recreational, economic and educational opportunities for local people and tourists alike. Upon completion in 1998, it will comprise three main sections and span over 600 miles of coastline, incorporating some 300 birding stops in nine wildlife refuges, eleven state parks, one national seashore, and several city and county preserves.

The variability of approaches used to define ecotourism has quite naturally given way to many comprehensive approaches used to understand the term. In her approach to the concept, Ziffer (1989) acknowledges the variety of descriptive terms such as nature travel, adventure travel, and cultural travel, which are largely activity based; and also the value-laden terms such as responsible, alternative, and ethical tourism, which underscore the need to consider impacts and the consequences of travel. Ziffer feels that nature tourism, while not necessarily ecologically sound in principle, concentrates more on the motivation and the behaviour of the individual tourist. Conversely, ecotourism is much more difficult to attain owing to its overall comprehensiveness (the need for planning and the achievement of societal goals). The defines Ecotourism as follows :

> a form of tourism inspired primarily by the natural history of an area, including its indigenous cultures. The ecotourist visits relatively undeveloped areas in the spirit of appreciation, participation and sensitivity. The ecotourist practises a non-consumptive use of wildlife and natural resources and contributes to the visited area through labour or financial means aimed at directly benefiting the conservation of the site and the economic well-being of the local residents. The visit should strengthen the ecotourist's appreciation and dedication to conservation issues in general, and to the specific needs of the locale. Ecotourism also implies a managed approach by the host country or region which commits itself to establishing and maintaining the sites with the participation of local residents, marketing them appropriately, enforcing regulations, and using the proceeds of the enterprise to fund the area's land management as well as community development.
>
> (Ziffer 1989 : 6)

Like Ziffer's, the following definition by Wallace and Pierce (1996 : 848) is also quite comprehensive, acknowledging the importance of a broad number of variables. To these authors, ecotourism is

> travel to relatively undisturbed natural areas for study, enjoyment, or volunteer assistance. It is travel that concerns itself with the flora, fauna, geology, and ecosystems of an area, as well as the people (caretakers) who live nearby, their needs, their culture, and their relationship to the land, it [*sic*] views natural areas both as 'home to all of us' in a global sense ('eco' meaning home) but 'home to nearby residents' specifically. It is envisioned as a tool for both conservation and sustainable development—especially in areas where local people are asked to forgo the consumptive use of resources for others.

Wallace and Pierce suggest that this tourism may be said to be true ecotourism if it addresses six principles :

(1) It entails a type of use that minimises negative impacts to the environment and to local people.

(2) It increases the awareness and understanding of an area's natural and cultural systems and the subsequent involvement of visitors in issues affecting those systems.

(3) It contributes to the conservation and management of legally protected and other natural areas.

(4) It maximises the early and long-term participation of local people in the decision-making process that determines the kind and amount of tourism that should occur.

(5) It directs economic and other benefits to local people that complement rather than overwhelm or replace traditional practices (farming, fishing, social systems, etc.).

(6) It provides special opportunities for local people and nature tourism employees to utilise and visit natural areas and learn more about the wonders that other visitors come to see.

Both Ziffer and Wallace and Pierce recognise that for Ecotourism to exist, it must strive to reach very lofty goals. By comparison, the Ecotourism Society advocates a much more general definition of the term, one that advocates a 'middle-of-the-road' or passive position (see Orams 1995), and one which is more easily articulated. This organisation defines ecotourism as 'responsible travel to natural areas which conserves the environment and improves the welfare of local people' (Western 1993 : 8). Preece *et al.* (1995) used the Australian National Ecotourism Strategy definition of ecotourism in their overview of biodiversity and ecotourism, which is also one that is quite general in nature. The strategy defines ecotourism as nature-based tourism that involves education and interpretation of the natural environment and is managed to be ecologically sustainable.

Although quite straightforward, these definitions leave much to the interpretation of the reader. As identified in Table 2.1, definitions of ecotourism over the years have emphasised different aspects of nature, relationships with local people, conservation

Table 2.1
Comparisons of Selected Ecotourism and Nature Tourism Definitions

Main principles of definition	*Definitions*														
	1	*2*	*3*	*4*	*5*	*6*	*7*	*8*	*9*	*10*	*11*	*12*	*13*	*14*	*15*
Interest in nature	✓	✓			✓	✓	✓	✓		✓	✓			✓	✓
Contributes to conservation			✓		✓	✓	✓	✓	✓	✓			✓	✓	✓
Reliance on parks and protected areas	✓		✓		✓	✓		✓	✓				✓	✓	✓
Benefits local people/long-term benefits			✓		✓	✓	✓		✓				✓	✓	✓
Education and study	✓	✓	✓			✓					✓			✓	✓
Low impact/non-consumptive					✓							✓	✓	✓	✓
Ethics/responsibility				✓					✓	✓					✓
Management					✓			✓			✓				✓
Sustainable								✓			✓			✓	✓
Enjoyment/appreciation	✓				✓									✓	
Culture	✓				✓									✓	
Adventure		✓													
Small scale												✓			✓

Source : (1) Ceballos-Lascuráin 1987; (2) Laarman and Durst 1987[b]; (3) Halbertsma 1988[b]; (4) Kutay 1989; (5) Ziffer 1989; (6) Fennell and Eagles 1990; (7) CEAC 1992; (8) Valentine 1993; (9) The Ecotourism Society; (10) Western; (11) Australian National Ecotourism Strategy; (12) Brandon 1996; (13) Goodwin 1996; (14) Wallace and Pierce 1996; (15) The present study.

Notes : *(a)* Variables ranked by frequency of response.

(b) Nature tourism definitions.

and preservation, and so on. The main issue confronting researchers who are bent on structuring definitions is either to include a whole series of principles and variables related to the term, or to try to isolate specific variables which can be used to best represent the overall concept. The fact of the matter is that, either implicitly or explicitly, such variables or principles need to be more effectively used to observe, measure and evaluate what is and what is not ecotourism.

In line with the previous discussion, Bottrill and Pearce (1995) point to the fact that the rich array of definitions of ecotourism have done little to clarify its meaning. Instead they opt for a means by which to operationalise ecotourism through the development of a set of measurable key elements for participant, operators and managers (see also Wallace and Pierce 1996, and their evaluation of ecotourism principles in Amazonas). In an analysis of 22 ecotourism ventures only five were classified as ecotourism using the following criteria: motivation (physical activity, education, participation), sensitive management, and protected area status. The authors submit that more work should follow to further define and modify the points and criteria raised. Their paper quite nicely addressed the need to move beyond definition to a position where ecotourism operators should be open to ethical and operational scrutiny by the public and other concerned stakeholders. This leads to the contentions of Miller and Kaye (1993 : 37), who suggest that 'the merits or deficiencies of ecotourism. . . are not to be found in any label *per se,* but in the quality and intensity of specific environmental and social impacts of human activity in an ecological system'.

Some researchers have discussed the placing of time on determining whether tourists are ecotourists or not. For example, Ballantine and Eagles (1994) suggested that ecotourists could be defined on the basis of an intention to learn about nature, an intention to visit undisturbed areas, and a commitment of at least 33 per cent of their time to the first two criteria. Blamey (1995) sees some inherent problems with the implementation of such a measure. The time factor advocated by Ballantine and Eagles may be applicable in the safari ecotourism settings of Africa, but could be more problematic in less structured ecotourism settings and situations. For instance, Blamey asks if a ten-minute guided nature tour qualifies as a day ecotourism visit. Yet one can't help but grapple for acceptable definitions of ecotourism, as Ballantine and Eagles and others have done; the same has occurred with the meaning of 'tourism' in the past, and similarly for many other social science disciplines. While the tourism literature has seen fit to define 'tourism' under many different circumstances—time, space, economics, whole systems models—the same will likely occur for ecotourism. It depends on who is operationalising the concept, and for what purpose. (See also Buckley 1994).

Given the foregoing discussion, I have elected to provide my own definition of ecotourism. In light of the review of a significant number of definitions, it is based on what is felt to be the most important aspects of the phenomenon and on the need to be concise in including such principles. It is as follows :

> Ecotourism is a sustainable form of natural resource-based tourism that focuses primarily on experiencing and learning about nature, and which is ethically managed to be low-impact, non-consumptive, and locally oriented (control, benefits and scale). It typically occurs in natural areas, and should contribute to the conservation or preservation of such areas.

Admittedly, this is more comprehensive than other definitions, but it strives to recognise that having been identified as a separate form of tourism, ecotourism must be classified and defined as such in order to maintain an element of homogeneity. This feeling is not expressed without some hesitation based on the writing of some other authors who imply that most people who demand ecotourism want a softer, easily accessible, front-country type of experience (Kearsley 1997 in Weaver 1998) and that the 'popular' form of ecotourism demands mechanised transport, easy accessibility, and a high level of services (Queensland Draft Ecotourism Strategy in weaver 1998). The relationship between this very soft form of ecotourism and other types of tourism has not been fully examined. The belief in this book is that much more than simply demand must go into the understanding of ecotourism and ecotourists. In an attempt to stay clear of this fine line, a harder stance on ecotourism is adopted. Furthermore, a stricter definition of ecotourism begs for the employment of measurable indicators in determining what is and is not ecotourism. (See Orams 1995 for a description of the hard-soft path ecotourism continuum.) An early example of this type of thinking can be seen through the efforts of Shores (1992), who identified the need for higher standards in the ecotourism industry through the implementation of scale to measure the level of achievement according to the principles of ecotourism. The scale ranges from 0 (travellers made aware of the fragility of the environment in a general capacity) to 5 (a trip where the entire system was operating in an environmental way).

The reader will most certainly recognise the absence of culture as a fundamental principle of ecotourism in the aforementioned definition. This definition views culture only inasmuch as the benefits from ecotourism accrue to local people, recognising that culture, whether exotic or not, is part of any tourism experience. If culture was a primary theme of ecotourism then it would be cultural tourism. There is no doubt that culture can be part of the ecotourism experience; the point is, however, that it is more likely to be a secondary motivation to the overall experience, not primary as in the case of nature and natural resources. For example, in a study completed by Fennell (1990) it was found that there was no statistically significant difference between the average Canadian traveller and ecotourists as regards many cultural attractions, including museums and art galleries, local festivals and events, and local crafts.

If one is to accept the fact that there currently exists an uneven base with which conceptually and empirically to determine differences in forms or types of nature tourists, it should thus be the task of researchers to focus on the isolation of variables by which to understand better the manifest and latent traits of these groups. Past research (see Bachert 1990) has combined education, experience, and learning into a comprehensive model of wilderness education. In this model learning is a key feature and is a variable which may also provide a basis from which to compare the on-site characteristics of the *nature tourism experience* over other familiar variables such as management, culture, economics and benefits. Other important variables to be considered (besides learning) may include the employment of skills or actions in the pursuit of the primary activity; the degree to which one subscribes to a strong or weak sense of what might be considered as 'biological or preservationist affect' (the emotional time that one has with plants, animals, or nature as a whole); and finally the degree of impact (consumptive to non-consumptive) caused by the type of tourism.

More specifically, learning relates to the need to gain knowledge on-site through interpretation and the information provided by guides and other facilitators. Further research in this area might endeavour to understand the differences or similarities between novelty and curiosity, and learning. In whalewatching, for example, many people just want to see a whale (novelty or curiosity), while conversely others want a more comprehensive learning-based whalewatching experience. In addition, future research may wish to examine the relationship between knowledge and learning in nature tourism. Knowledge can be thought of as information one applies to a situation, whereas learning is something that result from participation. There is little question that nature tourists learn from the experience, but it is important to view learning in terms of the primary motivation of the tourist. Second, skill may also be examined because it demonstrates that the application of skill is often employed at the expense of the environment rather than in some other benign fashion. Skill also relates to the previous discussion on primary motivation for participation in the nature tourism activity. There can be a strong case made for the assumption that ecotourism is learning based in its orientation, while other forms of nature tourism (e.g. mountain climbing) may be more skills based in their orientation. Third, biological affect may also provide some inroads in differentiating between nature tourists because it seeks to understand the perceptual place that flora, fauna, geological features, etc. occupy in the mind of the tourist. Consequently, the feelings of such users may dictate the forms of recreation participated in, and the effects of such activities on the natural world. This type of thinking relates to the work of Kellert (1985) on the attitudes of people towards animals on the basis of nine variables (negativistic and dominionistic as the most negative attitudes, versus naturalistic and ecologistic as the most positive). Kellert suggests that people and the activities they choose can be correlated with these values towards wildlife. Finally, consumptiveness of the activity (non-consumptive to consumptive) should be considered to illustrate that all forms of outdoor recreation and tourism have some type of impact—however insignificant—on the resource base, with some being less severe than others (consumptive forms of tourism include those that are said to consume resources, such as hunting and fishing).

Despite how the term *nature tourism* has evolved in the recent past, it is still difficult to equate it with activities that are more consumptive in their orientation (e.g. hunting). The activities that we now group under nature tourism, including adventure tourism, fishing, hunting, whalewatching, and ecotourism, might best be labelled *natural resource-based tourism*. This latter categorisation implies a element of use, which we know corresponds to any form of tourism that occurs outside and which relies specifically on the natural resource base. Furthermore, it is more analogous to the continuum of conservation (saving for use) and preservation (saving from use). Ecotourism, although it entails use, should apply more to the preservation end of this continuum, while hunting and fishing relate more to the aspect of conservation. This sentiment related to the work of Ewert (1997), who writes that 'resource-based' tourism includes a variety of tourism endeavours including ecotourism, adventure tourism, and indigenous tourism, and their various activities.

CASE STUDY 2.2

Nature Tourism in the USA

The Recreation Executive report of the US Forest Service (1994) illustrates that nature-based recreation trends as we approach the year 2000 show increases in many non-consumptive outdoor-activities. Outdoor photography is up 23 per cent, wildlife watching is up 16 per cent, backpacking is up 34 per cent, and day hiking is up 34 per cent. Also, the National Survey on Recreation and the Environment, a study conducted by the US federal government, concluded that of a number of outdoor recreation activities, birding, hiking and bakcpacking experienced the most significant growth in participation between 1982-83 and 1994-95. Birdwatching increased 155 per cent, hiking increased 93 per cent and backpacking increased 73 per cent. Conversely, hunting and fishing experienced negative growth over this period of time (-12 per cent and -9 per cent, respectively). Further to this, the White House Conference on Tourism in October 1995 indicated the following with respect to the non-consumptive use of birds:

Number of participants	$ 25 million
Retail sales	$ 5 billion
Wages and salaries	$ 4 billion
Full and part-time jobs	191,000
Tax revenues	
State sales	$ 306 million
State income	$ 74 million
Federal income	$ 516 million
Total economic output	$ 16 billion

Adventure Tourism or Ecotourism?

> A few hours of mountain climbing turn a villain and a saint into two rather equal creatures. Exhaustion is the shortest way to equality and fraternity—and liberty is added eventually by sleep.—Nietzsche

A close cousin that has developed alongside ecotourism is adventure travel, which in some circles is felt to subsume ecotourism. For example, in suggesting that ecotourism is a branch of adventure tourism, Dyess (1997 : 2) admits that he did not have a full appreciation of the heated disagreement that 'exists over the semantics of the two terms, as proponents of ecotourism and adventure travel strive to define and sanctify their own approach to travel'. In a general sense, differentiation between the two forms of travel can simply be based on the type of activity pursued (again, with respect to the primary motivation in participating in the activity). However, in cases where activities are broadly categorised as either ecotourism or adventure tourism, there may be problems, as evident in the following example. Tourism Canada has defined adventure tourism as 'an outdoor leisure activity that takes place in an unusual, exotic, remote or wilderness destination, involves some form of unconventional means of transportation, and tends to be associated with low or high levels of activity' (Canadian Tourism Commission 1995 : 5). The following is a list of adventure travel activities developed by the Canadian Tourism Commission (CTC) under this definition: (1) Nature Observation; (2) Wildlife Viewing (e.g. birding, whalewatching); (3) Water Adventure Products (e.g. canoeing, kayaking); (4) Land Adventure Products (e.g. hiking, climbing); (5) Winter Adventure Products (e.g. dog sledding, cross-country skiing); and (6) Air Adventure Products, including hot 'air ballooning, hand-gliding, air safaris, bungee jumping, and parachuting. The point to be made from this example is that both ecotourism and adventure tourism products may adhere to the CTC's definition, despite the fact that to many there is a clear distinction between nature observation (ecotourism) and kayaking (adventure tourism). Clearly, further analysis of these activities is required in order to detect similarities and differences. However, while activity is important (an outdoor pursuit) to identifying adventure activities, Priest (1990) writes that there must be an element of uncertainty associated with the event.

The answer to the question of how adventure and non-adventure tourism experiences like ecotourism differ may lie in the realm of social psychology, which examines why participation occurs from a cognitive and behavioural standpoint (instead of some arbitrary basis established on the basis of setting and other such variables). Both Ewert (1985) and Hall (1992) write that it is risk that plays a primary role in the decision to engage in adventurous activities. In addition, Hall suggests that it is the activity more than the setting that provides the dominant attraction for pursuit of adventure recreation and tourism. Two other factors in analysing one's motivation to engage in risk-related activities include challenge and skill, the fundamental variables behind Csikszentmihalyi's (1990) model of flow (see also Csikszentmihalyi and Csikszentmihalyi 1990). Individuals who are said to have reached a state of flow have matched their personal skills with the challenges of a particular activity. Flow includes a number of main elements as defined by Csikszentmihalyi. These include—

(1) *Total immersion into the activity*—This relates to the elimination of distractions that enable the person to lose touch with his or her surroundings.

(2) *Enhanced concentration*—A result of the previous factor that allows the participant to forget about the unpleasant tasks that may be associated with the activity.

(3) *Actions directed at fulfilling the goal*—The goals and objectives of the event are clearly understood by the participant, who knows how best to approach the situation.

(4) *The activity requires skill and challenge*—The relationship between these two variables is important in that if skill far exceeds challenge, boredom will result, whereas if challenge far exceeds skill, anxiety will result.

(5) *Flow involves control*—The participant exercises control over his or her movements and the situation, with a degree of anticipation of the events which will unfold.

(6) *A sense of transcendentalism*—Here the participant has the experience of transcending his or her physical being, as rooted on the face of the earth, to reach some higher

level of understanding or being. A sense of oneness with the surroundings or objects involved in the experience is felt.

(7) *The loss of time*—Frequently participants feel as though they have been involved for a short period of time (e.g. one hour), when in fact they have been involved for a long periods of time (e.g. four hours).

Csikszentmihalyi (1990) suggests that flow is not necessarily restricted to those who engage in adventurous activities, but also includes those, for example, playing chess or physicians engaged in surgery. According to Hall, then, it may be the desire or the enhanced desire to experience the state of flow that moves individuals to participate in risk or adventure-related activities.

To Quinn (1990), adventure lies deep within the spiritual, emotional, intellectual, and objective spheres of humanity; and is the eternal seduction of the hidden (Dufrene 1973 : 398). More specifically, Quinn argues that adventure is a desire for a condition that is absent within the individual. Under rather tenuous conditions, the individual must harbour doubt as to the adequacy of his or her ability. The further one attempts to go beyond one's perceived personal talents, the more intense the adventurous situation becomes. It is this element of unknown that led Einstein to suggest that 'the most beautiful and deepest experience a man can have is the sense of the mysterious' (cited in Mayur 1996). The adventure experience therefore is one that is not discrete but rather one that varies in intensity. The result is that in today's marketplace, tourists are able to select from a broad range of hard and soft adventure experiences, offering associated degrees of risk and uncertainty. According to Christiansen (1990), it is the task of the adventure tour operator to provide the client with an adequate perception of risk, while ensuring a high level of safety and security. This is accomplished through an accident-free history, good planning, and the maintenance of the highest level of leadership, skills and experience. Christiansen provides a good understanding of the difference between soft- and hard-core adventure experiences, as shown in Figure 2.3. The soft adventure activities in the figure are pursued by those interested in a perceived risk and adventure with little actual risk, whereas the hard adventure examples included are known by both the participant and the service provider to have a high level of risk (if, indeed a service provider is involved in the experience).

Risk	Soft adventure	Adventure	High adventure
High			— South Pole asking touring — Shark baiting — Sea kayaking — Storm skiing
		— Salman river — Raft trip — Himalaya trek — Mexico volcano climb	
Low	— Grand Canyon float trip — Mule trip to Grand Canyon bottom		

Adventure Level

Fig. 2.3 : Levels of risk in tour packages.

In related research the link between motivation and level of experience in mountain climbers was analysed by Ewert (1985), who based his research on the premise that the perception of danger is important in the experience of the risk recreation participant. From a survey of climbers at Mount Ranier National Park, Washington, he found that inexperienced climbers participated for recognition, escape, and social reasons. Conversely, the experienced climbers were motivated by more intrinsic reasons including exhilaration, challenge, personal testing, decision-making, and locus of control. The implications of the research are such that over time, climbers who continue with a risk recreation activity such as scuba-diving, mountain climbing, and speiunking (cave exploration) may require conditions that are less crowded, more rugged, and less controlled than their novice counterparts.

Fennell and Eagles (1990) focused on the element of risk in examining potential differences between adventure travel, Ecotourism and mass tourism in the framework shown in Figure 2.4. Here it is implied that preparation and training, known/unknown results and risks, and certainty and safety are all variables that may be used to differentiate between these forms of tourism. The figure demonstrates that the three kinds of activity are not mutually exclusive; ecotourism may share some elements of the other two experiences, while still remaining distinct from mass tourism and adventure tourism.

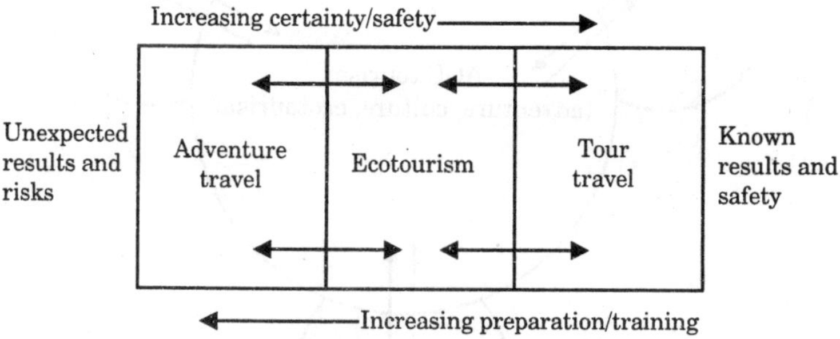

Fig. 2.4 : Tourism activity spectrum.

Figure 2.5 identifies the evolving relationship between three common AT products, namely ecotourism, adventure tourism and cultural tourism. As suggested earlier, the overlap between these three appears to have become stronger over the past few years, to the point where many studies, usually government or marketing ones (see CTC 1995 and Wight 1992), have considered them as almost completely synonymous (this phenomenon is represented by the acronym ACE in the figure). Depending on the setting and situation, ACE either expands or contracts to represent different concentrations of adventure, culture, and ecotourism, either in name alone or in product content. Those situations that are classed solely as ecotourism avoid the inclusion of conditions that relate to culture tourism or adventure tourism (or both). At the same time, there is the recognition that a continuum exists between hard- and soft-path ecotourism experiences (see Laarman and Durst 1987; Orams 1995). This figure (and the book) attempts to demonstrate that ecotourism should be considered as unique according to its function and role within the tourism marketplace, a stance which is based on the facts that (1) there is little empirical evidence demonstrating homogeneity between adventure tourism, culture tourism, and Ecotourism, and (2) there may be an associated dilution factor or effect on ecotourism if these three types of tourism merge into a combined form.

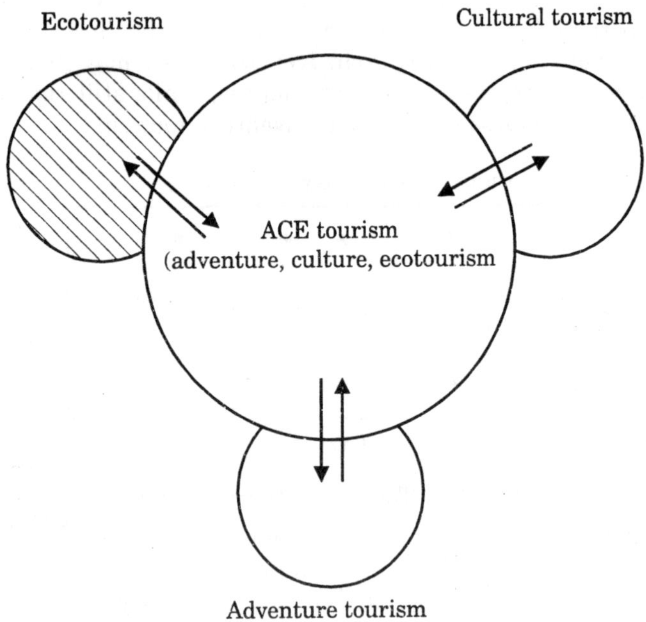

Fig. 2.5 : The changing face of ecotourism.

Tourist Typologies

The General Literature

Perhaps as a function of the tremendous demand for different types of travel experiences tourism has blossomed with a rich array of terms describing different types of vacation experiences in different settings, with virtually no research available to describe these various 'types' systematically (Boyd 1991 identifies some 90 types of tourism). Historically, tourism research has tended to concentrate not on tourism types, but rather on tourist types and the various individual traits, characteristics, motivations, needs, and so on of travellers. This has ultimately enabled both researchers and practitioners to better understand tourists on the basis of the types of experiences they seek, as individuals and groups. The following section briefly examine a number of pertinent motivational/behavioural and social/cultural typologies as a basis for understanding ecotourists.

Christaller quite effectively grasped the notion that, over time, a destination will play host to a rich variety of different types of travellers. He wrote :

> The typical course of development has the following pattern. Painters search out untouched unusual places to paint. Step by step the place develops as a so-called artist colony. Soon a cluster of poets follows, kindred to the painters; then cinema people, gourmets, and the *jeunesse dorée.* The place becomes fashionable and the entrepreneur takes note. The fisherman's cottage, the shelter huts become converted into boarding houses and hotels come on the scene. . . . Only the painters with a commercial inclination who like to do well in business remain; they capitalise on the good name of this former painter's corner and on the gullibility of tourists. More and more townsmen choose this place, now *en vogue* and advertised in the newspapers. . . At last the tourist agencies come with their package rate travelling parties; now, the indulged public avoids such places. At the same time, in other places the cycle occurs again; more and more places come into fashion, change their type, turn into everybody's tourist haunt.
>
> (Christaller 1963 : 103)

While tourist destinations were seen to be transformed under the influence of tourism, so did the type of traveller, either as a result of these changes or as responsible for initiating the changes within the region. Cohen (1972 : 172) commented, echoing Christaller, that 'Attractions and facilities which were previously frequented by the local population are gradually abandoned. As Greenwich Village became a tourist attraction, many of the original bohemians moved to the east Village'. Cohen used this as an analogy to demonstrate that travellers were inherently different on the basis of their relationship to both the tourist business establishment and host country. Accordingly, he grouped tourists into four categories, including organised mass tourists, individual mass tourists, explorers and drifters. This typology reflected a continuum such that the organised mass tourist is seen as the least adventure some with little motivation to leave the confines of his or her home environmental bubble. The drifter, in contrast, shunned the tourist establishment, searching for the most authentic travel experiences available.

Motivation, or the drive to satisfy inner physiological and psychological needs, has been fundamental to tourism researches interested in the 'why' of tourist travel. To Pearce (1982), there needs to exist a stronger emphasis in linking roles and motivations with social and environmental preferences of tourists, in order that destinations could be better matched with markets, travel expectations, and accommodation. Iso-Ahola (1982) suggested that travel motivation is purely psychological and not sociological in nature. He argued that people travel for basically two reasons: (1) to seek intrinsic rewards (novelty), and (2) to escape their everyday environments (escape). These two motivations may be either of a personal nature (personal troubles or failures) or interpersonal (related to co-workers, family, or neighbours). The amalgam of these elements is a four-cell matrix, where a single tourist could theoretically go through one or all aspects during the course of one trip.

MacCannell (1989) also considered the fundamental differences between traveller types in examining the social structure of tourist space based on 'front' and 'back' regions. Front regions are those readily experienced by tourists and places where hosts and guests regularly interact. Conversely, back regions are the preserve of the host and are essentially non-tourism oriented in their function. Tourists in search of authenticity penetrate back regions in the hope of acquiring real day-to-day mannerisms of residents. To what degree tourists are willing or able to penetrate back regions—in identified access zones of tourism areas—may be important to their achieving their overall purpose. Although these 'places' are actual locations in the conventional economic/geographical context, in the mind of the tourist or tourist group they hold special value in defining the travel experience. In general, these back regions are sociological.

Profiling the Ecotourist

Some of the earliest studies on ecotourism attempted to classify ecotourists on the basis of setting, experience, and group dynamics. For example, Kusler (1991) typified ecotourists as belonging to three main groups, including—

(1) *Do-it-yourself ecotourists*—Despite their relative anonymity, this group comprise the largest percentage of all ecotourists. These individuals stay in a variety of different types of accommodations, and have the mobility to visit any number of settings. Their experience, therefore, is marked by a high degree of flexibility.

(2) *Ecotourists on tours*—This group expects a high degree of organisation within their tour, and travel to exotic destinations (e.g. Antarctica).

(3) *School groups or scientific groups*—This group often become involved in scientific research of an organisation or individual, often stay in the same region for extensive periods of time, and are willing to endure harsher site conditions than other ecotourists.

Conversely, Lindberg (1991 : 3) emphasises the importance of dedication and time as a function of defining different types of ecotourists, including what tourists wish to experience from ecotourism, where they wish to travel, and how they wish to travel. Lindberg identified four basic types—

(1) *Hard-core nature tourists*—scientific researchers or members of tours specifically designed for education, removal of litter, or similar purposes;

(2) *Dedicated nature tourists*—people who take trips specifically to see protected areas and who want to understand local natural and cultural history;

(3) *Mainstream nature tourists*—people who visit the Amazon, the Rwandan gorilla park, or other destinations primarily to take an unusual trip; and

(4) *Casual nature tourists*—People who experience nature incidentally as part of a broader trip.

Consistent with the increase in ecotourism opportunities, and the associated typologies of tourists travelling on such trips, has been an increase in the volume of literature available on the ecotourist, with much of it focusing on presenting a profile of this tourist type. Initial studies decidedly pointed to the fact that the ecotourist was predominantly male, well educated, wealthy, and long-staying. For example, Wilson (1987 : 21) reported the following in researching 62 tourists visiting Ecuador :

> The male/female ratio was 52% to 48%, and the mean average age was 42. . . . Twenty-seven per cent earned a family income between US $ 30,000 to $ 60,000, before taxes annually. Approximately one-quarter earned more than $ 90,000 per year. About 30% had bachelors degrees, and a little over 10% had doctoral degrees.

Both Fennell and Smale (1992) and Reingold (1993) report similar results in their work on Canadian ecotourists. On average, the Canadian ecotourists in the Fennell and Smale study were 54 years of age, with the majority in the 60–69 age cohort. The sample was predominantly male (55 per cent), earned on average about CDN $ 60,000, with almost one-third and two-thirds having undergraduate and graduate degrees, respectively. According to these authors, this education is well above the national average of about 19 per cent and 4 per cent of Canadians having a bachelor's degree and graduate training, respectively. In Reingold's work, 24 per cent of Canadian ecotourists were 55 to 64 years of age, 36 per cent had annual incomes over $ 70,000, 65 per cent had a university degree; however, 64 per cent of the respondents of this study were female. This latter statistic goes against much of the previous research suggesting that males are slightly more representative of this group. The general outdoor recreation literature supports the fact that most participants—two-thirds or even three-quarters—are of the male gender (Hendee *et al.* 1990).

The studies involving ecotourists have been found to mirror related research on birdwatchers. For example, Applegate and Clark (1987) report that more men than women birdwatch and that they have strikingly high levels of affluence and education. More than 50 per cent of the respondents of their study had completed four years of college and had annual family incomes in excess of US $20,000. The findings of Kellert (1985) indicate that committed birders were 73 per cent male with an average age of 42. Committed birders were also far better educated (nearly two-thirds had college and/or graduate school education) and had higher incomes than respondents who did not birdwatch. As more studies of this nature surface in the future it will be interesting to see how the profile of the ecotourist changes (or stays the same) as a function of many variables, including the types of experiences and products offered to ecotourists, and the maturity of the industry.

Beyond an analysis of socio-demographics, Fennell and Smale (1992) directly compared the average Canadian tourist against a sample of ecotourists (based on the work of Fennell 1990). These researchers used the results of a 1983 Canadian study [Tourism Attitude and Motivation Study (CTAMS)] that analysed the general attitudes and benefits sought by a sample of 11,501 Canadian tourists. The questions used in the CTAMS were study duplicated and applied to a sample of ecotourists who had recently returned from a Costa Rican ecotourism trip between 1988 and 1989. Of 98 surveys mailed to the ecotourists (tourists were contacted by obtaining mailing lists of Canadian ecotour operators offering programmes in Costa Rica), 77 were returned and usable. The results of this study are found in Table 2.2.

In general, the findings illustrate that the benefits sought by ecotourists may be found in new, active, and adventuresome activities and involvements; while the Canadian population benefits were more strongly related to sedentary activity and family-related endeavours. Ecotourists were found to pursue attractions related to the outdoors (wilderness areas, parks and protected areas and rural areas); while attractions related to cities and resorts were more important to the average Canadian traveller. The implications of the research are such that they empirically demonstrate that there is indeed a difference between ecotourists and general travellers in terms of their trip-related needs and focus. Kretchman and Eagles (1990) and Williacy and Eagles (1990) followed the initial survey design of Fennell (1990) in comparing ecotourists in a variety of different settings. These studies were combined by Eagles (1992) in a comprehensive overview of the travel motivations of Canadian ecotourists. His results generally substantiate the results of Fennell and Smale (1992), above in suggesting that ecotourists are fundamentally different, in their travel motivations, from the average traveller.

As suggested earlier, an effective way in which to differentiate between types of tourists visiting particular regions is through an examination of various personal characteristics such as primary motives, benefits sought, and so on. Turnbull (1981), however, provides an interesting argument against such an

Table 2.2
Relative Importance of Selected Attractions and Benefits to Canadian Travellers and Ecotourists[a]

Variable	*General population*		*Canadian ecotourists*	
	Mean[b]	*s.d.*	*Mean*	*s.d.*
Important benefits to ecotourists[c]				
Experiencing new and different lifestyles	2.67	1.02	1.95	0.78
Trying new foods	2.85	0.99	2.43	0.82
Being physically active	2.36	1.03	1.88	0.92
Visiting historical places	2.71	1.04	2.35	0.74
Seeing as much as possible	2.01	0.99	1.77	0.81
Being daring and adventuresome	2.91	0.98	2.62	1.01
Meeting people with similar interests	2.08	0.94	1.91	0.71
Important benefits to population[c]				
Watching sports	3.16	0.96	3.84	0.37
Visiting friends and relatives	1.83	1.03	3.25	0.82
Doing nothing at all	2.86	1.00	3.72	0.60
Being together as a family	1.66	0.98	2.92	1.04
Reliving past good times	2.46	1.06	3.36	0.79
Visiting places my family came from	2.70	1.16	3.45	0.84
Feeling at home away from home	1.81	0.91	2.64	0.93
Having fun and being entertained	1.95	0.88	2.72	0.94

(Continue)

Important attractions to ecotourists[c]				
Wilderness areas	2.34	1.09	1.06	0.37
National parks and reserves	2.21	1.01	1.14	0.35
Rural areas	2.34	0.94	1.49	0.60
Mountains	2.34	1.07	1.50	0.66
Lakes and streams	2.05	0.99	1.57	0.59
Historic sites and parks	2.37	1.01	2.05	0.81
Cultural activities	2.66	0.97	2.32	0.87
Oceanside	2.15	1.07	1.97	0.78
Important attractions to population[c]				
Indoor sports	2.98	0.94	3.85	0.35
Amusement and theme parks	2.74	0.99	3.80	0.54
Nightlife and entertainment	2.72	1.04	3.70	0.56
Gambling	3.61	0.69	3.96	0.34
Shopping	2.45	1.01	3.14	0.74
Resort areas	2.56	1.01	3.26	0.82
Big cities	2.94	0.93	3.39	0.69
Beaches for swimming/sunning	2.34	1.10	2.79	0.96
Predictable weather	2.11	0.97	2.40	0.81
Live theatre and musicals	2.99	1.01	3.21	0.91

Source : Fennell and Smale 1992.

Notes : *(a)* Differences between general population and ecotourists are statistically significant at 0.05 level.

(b) Scale: 1 = 'very important'; 4 = 'not at all important.

(c) Attractions/benefits are in descending rank order based on magnitude of difference between groups.

approach. He suggests that although on the surface nature tourists travelling to Africa state that it is primarily the animals that bring them to the game parks of East Africa, on the basis of his observations he feels that the reasons for visiting Africa run much deeper. As an anthropologist, Turnbull believes that perhaps latently it is also the 'Africa' and the 'Kilimanjaro' that bring such tourists to this setting. In essence, he believes that people want to tap into their distant past when humans had a much stronger relationship with animals, seeing them as something more than just prey to be hunted, and it is to experience something of this relationship that is really desired by present-day tourists. He states that the tourists :

> expect an indivisible, natural whole made up of both human and animal components. But unless they are unusually lucky this is not what tourists find on the organised safari. All that is observed is man-made game parks devoid of the herders and hunters who used to live there as an indispensable part of the ecosystem. (Turnbull 1981 : 34)

This theory gives us another means by which to further examine the intergroup differences that exist between various forms of tourism (i.e. ecotourists and non-ecotourists), but also the intragroup differences (i.e. soft-path ecotourists and hard-path ecotourists) as well. We cannot blindly accept the notion that ecotourists are one homogeneous group; instead, as outlined above, they may be differentiated on the basis of many variables.

CONCLUSION

Despite the volume of literature that has emerged on the topic of ecotourism, it is clearly at an early stage of development, as is our understanding of how ecotourism differs from other types of tourism. More research is needed to help formulate definitions acceptable to those working in the field, to help overcome this critical absence of focus. The literature points to the fact that ecotourism is one aspect of nature oriented tourism, which includes many other types of tourism and outdoor recreation, both consumptive and non-consumptive. Ecotourism is said to relate to adventure travel only inasmuch as it shares similar environmental settings. Differentiation between these two forms of tourism must be done on the basis of social psychology. Finally, more studies are needed to further our understanding of who the ecotourist is, especially in relation to other types of tourists.

3

The Foundations of Ecotourism

THE EXPLOITATION OF THE NATURAL WORLD

Natural Resources

People use resources to accomplish ends in a variety to work and leisure settings. In the workplace, workers make use of other people (human resources) as well as facilities and equipment (physical resources), and in some cases the natural environment (natural resources), to accomplish their various tasks. During travel the same holds true, but the motivational focus alters to incorporate the use of such resources, independently or in combination, to satisfy a range of personal needs and expectations.

Zimmerman (1951 : 15) noted that resources 'are not, they become; they are not static but expand and contract in response to human actions'. That is, elements of the resource base such as trees, water, rocks, etc. do not become resources until they are capable of satisfying human needs. Zimmerman referred to elements of the environment that do not have human utility as 'neutral stuff'. The further humankind delves into the realm of the natural world, the more this neutral stuff becomes transformed into resources. Culture also has an effect on who uses such resources, and to what degree. For example, oil becomes a resource if people endeavour to develop the knowledge and ability to extract it, and combine it with the technology required to build the implements we use for work, leisure and survival (cars, furnaces, and so on). Resources, therefore, are dynamic both in space and time and are very much related to the perception of their worth to a particular person or society, as suggested by

Mitchell (1989 : 2): 'Natural resources are defined by human perceptions and attitudes, wants, technological skills, legal, financial and institutional arrangements, as well as by political systems.... Resources, to use Zimmerman's words, are subjective, relative and functional'.

The pursuit of touristic needs occurs along a broad physical site development continuum, from those settings that have been substantially modified by humans to pristine environments with very little human intervention. Chubb and Chubb (1981) suggest that the dividing line between what is developed and what is undeveloped is contingent upon one's perception of the meaning of the word 'developed' in relation to the tourism setting. Developed resources include highways, facilities, sewerage, buildings, and so on, that facilitate the use of a given area. Conversely, undeveloped resources may be found both in urban and wilderness environments but the degree to which they are recognised as such is individual dependent and perhaps situation dependent. These authors outline seven different types of undeveloped resources as they apply to outdoor recreation (and hence tourism). Although independent, each of the following must be envisioned as integrated, as it is the combination of elements of the environment that structure our tourism experiences.

- *Geographic location*—The characteristics of space that determine the conditions, in association with other variables, for participation (e.g. skiing).
- *Climate and weather*—Determined by latitude and elevation relative to large landforms, mountains, ocean currents, and high-altitude air currents. Along with geology, climate is the prime controller of the physical environment, affecting soils, vegetation, animals and the operation of geomorphological processes such as ice and wind.
- *Topography and landforms*—The general shape of the surface of the earth (topography) and the surface structures that make some geographical areas unique (landforms). A landform region is a section of the earth's surface characterised by a great deal of homogeneity among types of landforms.
- *Surface materials*—The nature of the materials making up the earth's surface, including rocks, fossils, minerals, soil, sand, etc.

- *Water*—This substance plays a critical role in determining the type and level of outdoor recreational participation in ocean and sea environments as well as freshwater settings (lakes, rivers and wetlands).
- *Vegetation*—Vegetation refers to the total plant life or cover in an area. Recreation quite often is dependent on plant life directly (tourists taking pictures of unique plant species), or indirectly (trees acting as a wind barrier for skiers).
- *Fauna*—Animals can play a significant role for recreational activities that are both consumptive and non-consumptive in nature. Forms of consumptive recreation view wildlife from the notion that animals have a utilitarian or dominionistic function (e.g. fishing, hunting, etc.). Non-consumptive recreation on the other hand has a softer impact on the resource base (e.g. birdwatching).

It should be noted that these resources may act either as catalysts in facilitating and drawing people to a tourist region or as constraints to visitation. A recent case in point is Montserrat. This small island state in the Caribbean is blessed with an abundance of natural features in its 102 km^2, and these usually act as a catalyst to draw people to this destination. Given its relative abundance of natural and climatic features, Montserrat has been referred to as an excellent example of a region where ecotourism may prosper (Reynolds 1992; Weaver 1995). However, in 1997 the tourism industry took a turn for the worse when the island's dormant volcano erupted, leaving the island, and the island's economy, in a critical state. Natural disaster such as this have not only an immediate effect but also a long-term effect, as Weaver (1995 : 601) writes in anticipating the fate of Montserrat's tourism industry :

> The inevitable hurricanes and earthquakes of the future will periodically curtail ecotourism by damaging not only the physical environment, but the roads, hiking trails, and viewing platforms upon which the sector depends. Furthermore, a prolonged moratorium on tourist activity may be necessary in some areas as the environment recovers from a natural disaster.

The Earth's Bounty

In an influential treatise on the historical roots of our present-day ecological dilemma, White (1971) argues strongly for the notion that, where formerly humankind was part of nature, over the past several hundred years our species has become the exploiter of nature and natural resources. The strength behind this conviction lies in how Western Christianity and capitalism have polarised humankind and nature by insisting that 'it is God's will that man exploit nature for his proper ends' (White 1971 : 12). Historical accounts charge that many scientists of the Middle Ages and Renaissance periods were tempered by this Christian philosophy. During the great scientific renewals of the 1500s and 1600s, a mechanistic and static perception of nature developed, replacing the passive mystic and organic views of earlier times. The push was towards a type of science that had designs on enlarging the bounds of the human empire in the endless pursuit of knowledge and control in order to 'regain the level of understanding and power once enjoyed in the Garden of Eden' (Bowler 1993 : 85).

Another significant element that contributed to humankind's dominance over nature was fear of the unknown. Although scientists in medieval times had begun to unravel some of nature's mysteries, their lack of understanding of the intricacies and interconnectedness of the environment contributed to the feeling that marginal places—such as the wilderness—were areas that had to be subdued (Short 1991). Land and animals were dichotomised as either settled or savage, cultivated or uncultivated, domesticated or wild. Through Christian eyes, wilderness areas (forests, bogs, and the like) were settings that contained pagans exercising pagan rites. In order to bring about religious order, such lands had to be cut down and cleansed. The abundant body of literature that exists on human—wilderness relations illustrate that there is no specific material object or space that one can identify as being 'wilderness' (Nash 1982). Wilderness is a concept that produces specific feelings or moods within people, and occurs within one's mind as a perceived place. Such a place may be wilderness to one, but not to another. This attitude prevailed in the Puritan mind as the first settlers set foot on North American soil. The new settlers were religiously and morally obligated to spend the bulk of their time in work-related activities. Leisure was severely curtailed and strictly regulated in accordance with religious protocol. The implications for nature were such that the wilderness represented both a challenge and an obstacle to a sustained European colony within the New World.

Socio-economically, significant changes were occurring in Britain during the period 1750 to 1850. It was a time of massive transformation and development of British industry by the use of new technologies and the circuit of industrial capital, which inevitably contributed to drastic changes in the leisure patterns of British citizens (a rural-to-urban population shift, longer working hours, and the exploitation of workers). Emerging within Britain and later in North America during the early 1800s was a progressive human attitude geared towards development that emphasised the following (Short 1991) : (1) the creation of liveable places and usable spaces (houses, industry); (2) the regarding of wilderness areas as waste and desolation; (3) the idea that civilised human society gave significance to the world; and (4) the conquest of wilderness as a signal of human achievement.

CASE STUDY 3.1

Natural History Travel in Shetland, Scotland

Butler (1985) writes that up to 1750 the Highlands and Islands of Scotland were virtually *terra incognita* to the people of the rest of Britain. The Shetland Islands were no exception. However, as a consequence of its unique location, Shetland provided both a geographical and a cultural link between Scandinavia to the east and Great Britain to the south. Flinn (1989) suggests that before 1850 the people who travelled to Shetland were artists, geologists, naturalists, physicists and surveyors. In 1814 Sir Walter Scott visited Shetland and used the region as the setting for his novel *The Pirate*. As Simpson (1983) illustrates, Scott's novels suffused a romance and drama of the book's region in the minds of the readers, compelling them to visit such places. In 1832 an ironmaster and naturalist, G.C. Atkinson, travelled to Shetland, perhaps as a result of Scott's influence. He wrote, 'I have long felt the greatest interest in descriptions of novel and extraordinary scenery and of the inhabitants and natural productions of regions that have been little known, either from their difficulty in attainment. . .or from their being so near'. By 1850, Flinn contends, the nature of the Shetland visitor was somewhat different. He wrote, 'by 1859 Shetland had a frequent steamer service from the south during the summer months, and a trunk road system which made the islands more accessible to tourists of a less hardy and enterprising breed' (*ibid.*: 235). Tourism, it appears, had displaced the traveller bent on exploration and challenge with a breed less willing to endure the hardships of travel.

The Roots of Conservationism

As the modification of the natural world began to intensity, it was beginning to be understood in France and Britain that deforestation was a predominant cause of soil erosion and poor productivity. These discoveries prompted early attempts at conservation in Britain, and in British India, where forested lands were set aside for the purpose of shipbuilding. Such areas were referred to as *conservancies,* and the foresters in charge of these areas as *conservators* (Pinchot 1947). There is evidence, however, to suggest that reforestation policies were being implemented in Britain in the seventeenth century (Bowler 1993).

In North America, conservationism evolved on three fronts (Ortolano 1984). The first involved the view that conservation should entail the maintenance of *harmony* between humankind and nature, the second that conservation related to the *efficient* use of resources. The final perception was that conservation—preservation—could ideally be attained from the standpoint of religion and *spirituality.* This latter view of conservation engendered a philosophy with the aim of saving resources *from* use rather than saving them *for* use (Passmore 1974). Each of these perspectives is discussed in further detail below.

Harmony

In the United States, a former Minister to Turkey and key founder of the Smithsonian Institution, George Perkins Marsh, became an instrumental figure in illustrating to Americans that their actions (commerce and lifestyles) were uniquely potent. Marsh wrote that:

> The earth is fact becoming an unfit home for its noblest inhabitant, and another era of equal human crime and human improvidence. . .would reduce it to such a condition of impoverished productiveness, of shattered surface, of climatic excess, as to threaten the depravation, barbarism, and perhaps even extinction of the species. (Bowler 1993 : 319)

His *Man and Nature,* originally published in 1864, recognised that in the changing conditions of nineteenth century America, harmony between human influences (modifications) and the natural world could be achieved only through society's commitment to a moral and social responsibility to future generations. (This view was rekindled over eighty years later by the land ethic philosophies of Aldo Leopold.) Marsh identified the collective power of large corporations as the factor most responsible for the increasing negative impacts to the natural world. Politically, the accountability of the large firms did not become an issue until the turn of the century. The Roosevelt administration recognised that the federal government had been too generous in granting favours (leases; land rights, etc.) to such corporations (Hays 1959), and as a result attempted (1) to find an adequate means of controlling and regulating corporate activities; and (2) to resist the efforts of corporations to exploit the natural resources of the nation on their own behalf.

At the time, changing technology, industrialisation, urbanisation, population growth and transportation all contributed to the feeling that the American frontier was diminishing. This fact was most emphatically illustrated by the direct relationship between the advancement of the transcontinental railroad and the decline of American buffalo. The combination of a loss of habitat and the shooting of buffalo for sport (from the trains themselves) contributed significantly to the downfall of this species. Space was also a critical factor in the frontier mentality. Americans had reached the supposed limits of their 'manifest destiny' by encountering the Pacific to the west, Canada to the north and Mexico to the south. In Canada, the frontier attitude lingered on because of the challenges encountered in settling and harnessing the conditions of the north.

Efficient Use

By the beginning of the twentieth century, Americans were ripe to exercise concern over the fate of their resource base (Nash 1982). The concept of conservation became a vehicle to represent the new frontier; the means by which American society could maintain vitality and prosperity. However, despite conservationism's apparent simplicity—the wise use of natural resources—fierce debate surfaced over how such resources ought to be utilised, if at all.

The efficient use of resources perspective represented the opposite end of the conservation spectrum from the perspective of preservationism, and was championed by an American by the name of Gifford Pinchot. Pinchot developed a concept of natural resources for the greatest good of the greatest number for the longest time (Herfindahl 1961). More directly, conservation was to engender direct control over natural resources on the basis of three principles (Pinchot 1910): (1) to develop the continent's existing natural resources for the benefit of the people who live there now; (2) to prevent the waste of natural resources; and (3) to develop and preserve resources for the benefit of the many, and not merely for the profit of a few.

This philosophy of conservation, at the very least, recognised the need for people to acknowledge that natural resources were finite. Industry and the individuals both had to be more accountable for their actions under the rationale that what was utilised today might have repercussions for those in the future. From this standpoint, conservationism was indeed progressive, as suggested by Hays (1959 : 264) :

> The broader significance of the conservation movement stemmed from the role it played in a transformation of a decentralised, non-technical, loosely organised society, where waste and inefficiency ran rampant, into a highly organised, technical, and centrally planned and directed social organisation which could meet a complex world with efficiency and purpose.

Spirituality

A more romantic view of wilderness was developing in response to the technological and industrialised transformation of Britain and Europe. Based on the works of Erasmus Darwin, Wordsworth, Coleridge, and Carlyle, Romanticism developed from the more regressive view that society had declined from past, more harmonious times. Romanticism embodied a deeper spirituality and awareness that a simpler life was attainable without the complications of a society blemished by materialism, and could be accomplished under the following conditions (Short 1991): (1) untouched spaces had the greatest significance; (2) these spaces had a purity which human contact degrades; (3) wilderness was a place of deep spiritual significance; and (4) the conquest of nature was a fall from grace.

The first proponent of the Romantic philosophy within North American society was Ralph Waldo Emerson, who had met and been inspired by the romantic poets of Britain in the early 1830s. The main doctrine of Emerson's interpretation of Romanticism surrounded the belief that although mankind was firmly rooted to the physical world, people had the ability to 'transcend' this condition (spiritually) in searching for and achieving deeper philosophical truths. Emerson's transcendentalism was a spiritual doctrine of humankind and nature. To Emerson, humankind was divided into materialists and idealists, with the first class founded upon experience and the second on consciousness. The materialists were to insist on facts, history, circumstances, and animal instincts; the idealists on the power of thought, will, and miracle. His major work, *Nature* (1835), had a significant impact on many other writers to follow, including Henry David Thoreau, Herman Melville, John Burroughts, Walt Whitman and John Muir.

Nature in North American society thus began to hold and inspire a small but articulate core of advocates paving a clear path out of the downward-spiralling pattern of a materialistic, consumptive society. Although the works of Emerson were largely idealistic, the transcendentalist movement also provided the rationale for practical change within American society. Thoreau, for example, campaigned to have the US government establish national preserves for the purpose of ensuring the future well-being of animals (Finch and Elder 1990). Such a call was well ahead of its time, as the United States did not endeavour to establish protected areas until a number of years later.

The emergence of a second tier of conservation (environmentalism or the green movement) occurred in the 1960s in response to the rapid and overwhelming increase in the impact of technology in society. Publications such as Rachel Carson's *Silent Spring* were effective in calling attention to the insidious effects of chemical use within society. In addition, ecology and the growing importance of science had begun to become institutionalised and gain acceptance as a mechanism to evaluate many social and ecological ills of the time. Bowler (1993) writes that the most militant supporters of the environmental movement opposed the entire economic structure of society in favour of a reversal to a simpler, more natural state. Examples of organisations/movements advocating a more radical approach to environmentalism include Greenpeace, Deep Ecology (founded by Arne Naess), and the Eco-Feminist Connection, which is believed to go deeper than Deep Ecology in addressing the man-centred approach to development within society and the fact that human females best represent the close time with Mother Nature. Those environmentalists considered less militant called for the protection of selected parcels of land that held natural and cultural significance, with the request that industrialisation and development occur outside the realm of such areas. According to Bowler, a fundamental difference existed between the two camps. Those less enthusiastic (i.e. those in favour of the development of nature reserves) recognised that minor changes could occur within the current system, while the most enthusiastic environmentalists wanted to destroy the existing social order. It is the former group that, in a practical sense, has made the most significant gains in the context of the global arena. Ecotourism, to some, is merely an extension of this philosophy of 'working within the system' and one that, at least conceptually, attempts to knit the elements of economy and ecology together (via parks) through the tenets of environmentalism and sustainable development (see Chapter 1).

Parks and Protected Areas

The concept of 'park' is one that is firmly established within civilisation (Smith 1990a; Wright 1983). The Greeks and Romans met at designated open spaces (*agorae*), while in medieval times the European nobility used their private lands as hunting reserves. With very few unmodified open spaces left in Britain by the nineteenth century, the concept of 'park' began to be recognised as a means by which to secure outdoor recreation opportunities in the countryside. To accommodate demand, the nobility began to lease open space for summer and winter recreation of all classes within British society. The importance of parks was more formally established by the Municipal Corporations Act in 1835, allowing for the creation of municipal parks and for the secure right of public recreation.

In Britain, the parks movement stemmed largely from the response of the British public to the effects of urbanisation, pollution, and loss of leisure equated with the Industrial Revolution. The same could not be said for the evolution of parks in Canadian society. Wright (1983 : 45) illustrates that urban parks in Canada were created to satisfy a concept rather than a reality:

the establishment of local parks in the 1850-1880 period in Ontario was merely the continuation in Canada of a programme and philosophy adopted in Britain and maintained by the elite in their own environment, not because the conditions in Canada demanded its implementation but because the colonial settles wished to preserve the values and beliefs inherited from their ancestral homes.

Ontario was the first of the provinces in Canada to enact legislation governing municipal park development in 1883 (Eagles 1993). This occurred at a time when there was a heightened awareness in North America of the need for parkland. The world's first national park had been created in Yellowstone in 1872, and Canada's first national park was to be created two years after Ontario's municipal legislation in 1885.

Parks and protected areas (the terminology used in this section to refer to public lands held in trust with both a recreation/tourism and conservation/preservation mandate, and owned and usually operated by a public agency) have a certain mystique to travellers interested in some of the best representative natural regions or countries. In fact, it was Johst (1982) who suggested that visitation to parks may increase by virtue of their designation as such. Simply stated parks and protected areas often times generate more recreational use simply because they are recognised as parks [although McCool (1985) contests this point].

Harroy (1974) has shown that Yellowstone was created to satisfy a broad mandate of concerns that had emerged from the United States' frontier mentality. Foremost, the park was set up to prevent the exploitation of wildlife and the environment, for the purpose of recreation, and finally as a means of scientific study. Canada's first national park, Banff, on the other hand, was established for political and economic reasons, including the generation of tourism dollars (largely from the therapeutic and recreational benefits of the hot springs) for the purpose of offsetting the cost of building the transcontinental railway (Lothian 1987). Banff's popularity quickly escalated to the point where the park was absorbing a wide variety of recreational demands including fishing, horseback riding, hunting, mountain climbing, and so on, but also other resource demands such as mining, logging, grazing, and a town site. Rollins (1993) suggests that as a case study, Banff represented the types of problems that

Parks Canada has had to address over the past 110 years regarding the management of natural features, with many conflicting stakeholders harbouring consumptive and non-consumptive designs on the use of park resources.

In Canada and many countries around the world, national parks are broadly mandated with the dual purposes of protecting representative natural areas of significance, and encouraging public understanding, appreciation and enjoyment. Their main focus, therefore, is to balance recreational use with the protection of unique physiographic land and water regions. Historically, the preservation ideal within parks was not fully developed or emphasised. However, as the system of protected areas continues to grow (as illustrated by the increasing circles over time in Figure 3.1), park management philosophies have become better integrated, recognising that parks do not exist as ecological islands, but must be managed according to environmental conditions both inside and outside their boundaries (Dearden 1991).

The debate surrounding the threats to parks and park management has prompted some researchers to acknowledge a situation of crisis in the national parks in the United States due to both internal and external factors (Chase 1987), and even that national parks in their current form are not sufficient to remain effective in the future (Janzen cited in Chase 1989). Janzen illustrates, using the African game parks as an example, that the establishment of wilderness lands has been, in many cases, self-defeating in that they slowly become consumed by poaching and adjacent farmers. To Janzen, a preferable approach would be to view the national park as an agent of social change, where local people would be stakeholders within the park and their social and economic activities (e.g. tourism and farming) would be ecologically sustainable.

Lovejoy (1992) writes that today, parks serve a variety of purposes but also face a number of pressures. He cites fertiliser use infiltrating the park environment from adjacent lands, the temptation of local people to use park resources, self-serving political interests that influence park management, overpopulation, and habitat fragmentation as frequent dilemmas challenging park managers. Worldwide, though, Lovejoy suggests that increased tourism visitation stand as one of the most

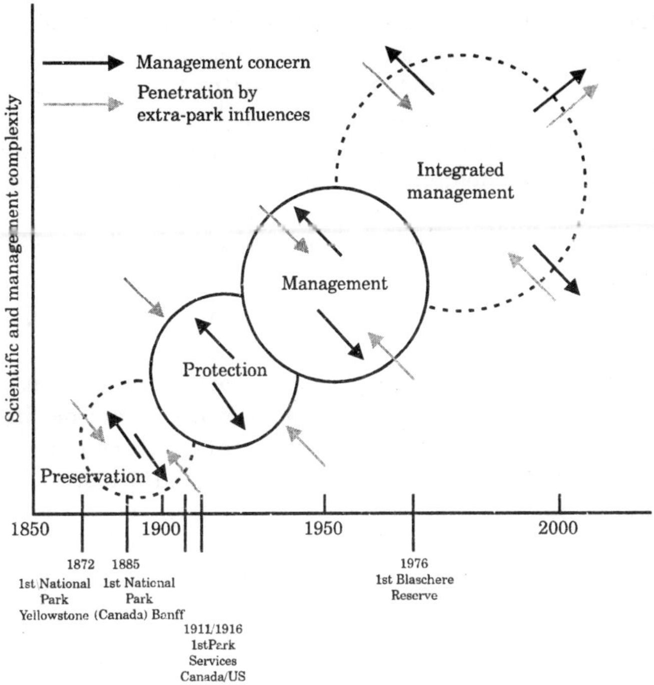

Fig. 3.1. : The evolving role of parks.

persistent problems facing parks and protected areas. He identified Yosemite and Yellowstone National Parks in the United States as examples particularly representative of this problem. Yosemite is overused during the summer, and the Yellowstone authorities, despite the parks integration with surrounding communities, were criticised—by those with business enterprises in or around the park—for allowing the extensive fires of 1989 to burn, which in turn affected the tourism industry. Parks, therefore, have come to rely on tourism as a means by which to generate income from a growing world population with increasing disposable time, financial well-being and personal mobility.

The problems between parks and local populations outlined above are mirrored by Hough (1988), who feels that restrictions of access to traditionally used resources, and the disruption of local cultures and economies by tourists, etc., have led to hostility, resentment, and damage to park property. He identifies eight key obstacles to effective management of park-people relationships, namely the institutional structure of national parks (i.e. the concept of park and their policy structures); the lack of trust between local people and park authorities; the lack of communication between parks and local people; the large number of different stakeholders in the park; the polarisation of power between government and local populations; the risk and uncertainty in entering into discussions aimed at reducing conflict; the enforcement of agreements between the park and local population; and the lack of opportunity for all to participate in the decision-making process.

In general, the threats to parks and parks management have, according to Dearden and Rollins (1993), evolved over time, having been primarily internal but now more external in their orientation. This evolution has coincided with the belief that the roles of parks have changed significantly from when they were developed initially (at least in Canada), at which time the primary role was to cater to recreationists. This is no longer the case, at least in theory, however, with the recent changes to the Canadian Parks Act in 1988 to underscore the importance of ecological functioning of parks above the recreational component.

Section 5(1.2) of the 1988 amendments suggests that maintenance of ecological integrity through the protection of natural resources is to be the first priority when considering park zoning and visitor use in the management plan (Canada, Parliament 1993). Park zoning is one of the key planing and management tools within parks. Zones are established on the basis of natural resources and their need for protection, and capacity to absorb recreational involvement. An overview of the theoretical basis for zoning in national parks in Canada (Environment Canada 1990) is illustrated as follows (for more of a history on the development of outdoor recreation land classification, the reader should consult the US Outdoor Recreation Resource Review Commission reports of the early 1960s) :

- *Zone 1: Special Preservation*—Specifies areas or features which deserve special preservation because they contain or support unique, rare, or endangered features or the best examples of natural features. Access and use will be strictly controlled or may be prohibited altogether. No motorised access or humanmade facilities will be permitted.

- *Zone 2: Wilderness*—Extensive areas which are good representations of each of the natural history themes of the park and which will be maintained in a wilderness state. Only certain activities requiring limited primitive visitor facilities appropriate to a wilderness experience will be allowed. Limits will be placed on numbers of users. No motorised access will be permitted. Management actions will ensure that visitors are dispersed.
- *Zone 3: Natural Environment*—Areas that are maintained as natural environments, and which can sustain, with a minimum of impairment, a selected range of low-density outdoor activities with a minimum of related facilities. Non-motorised access will be preferred. Access by public transit will be permitted. Controlled access by private vehicles will be permitted only where it has traditionally been allowed in the past.
- *Zone 4: Outdoor Recreation*—Limited areas that can accommodate a broad range of education, outdoor recreation opportunities and related facilities in ways that respect the natural landscape and that are safe and convenient. Motorised access will be permitted and may be separated from non-motorised access.
- *Zone 5: Park Services*—Towns and visitor centres in certain existing national parks which contain a concentration of visitor services and support facilities as well as park administration functions. Motorised access will be permitted.

Rollins (1993) illustrates, however, that zoning is primarily natural resource based, and does not define the types or levels of recreational opportunities that can occur within such regions of the park. Visitor management within parks in North America is addressed through a number of preformed planning and management frameworks, including the Recreation Opportunity Spectrum (ROS), the Limits of Acceptable Change (LAC), and the Visitor Activity Management Process (VAMP). The former two are American and the latter is Canadian.

CASE STUDY 3.2

Last Mountain Lake National Wildlife Area

This Saskatchewan wildlife area is significant in that 1,013 hectares of it was designated as the first federal bird sanctuary in North America on June 8, 1887. According to the Canadian Wildlife Service (1995), over 280 bird species have been recorded at Last Mountain Lake during peak migration, including 50,000 cranes, 450,000 geese, and several hundred thousand ducks. In addition, the area provides habitat for 9 of Canada's 36 vulnerable, threatened, and endangered birds, including the whooping crane and peregrine falcon. Last Mountain Lake has been designated as a Wetland of International Importance along with approximately 30 other sites in Canada and 700 locations worldwide (as of 1995). Although conservation is the primary purpose within the area, other, more consumptive activities such as hunting and fishing are allowed in adjacent areas under strict regulation.

Only about 2 per cent of Canada's land mass is protected within the national parks system. National parks, though, represent only one of the many systems in Canada developed to safeguard biophysical resources (others include provincial parks, wildlife reserves, environmentally sensitive areas, areas of natural and scientific interest, biosphere reserves, and world heritage sites). However, all told, these protected areas represent between 6 and 7 per cent of the Canadian landscape, but only 2.6 per cent if one excludes protected areas where logging, mining, and hunting are nevertheless allowed (Rollins and Dearden 1993). Furthermore, it has taken some 110 years to fully establish 38 national parks in Canada. Critics of the parks system are quick to point to the fact that Canadians are moving far too slowly in developing the country's network of parks. In 1987, the Brundtland Commission (the World Commission on Environment and Development) set a standard of 12 per cent for all countries in terms of the amount of territory that needed to be established as parks and protected areas. Such a standard is believed to be a level that would ensure a degree of protection for all the earth's major physiographic regions. Canada's commitment to this standard came in the form of the Green Plan (Canada Government, 1990). For the purpose of protected areas, some of the goals outlined within the plan include the following: (1) to establish at least five new national parks by 1996; and (2) to negotiate agreements for the remaining 13 parks required to complete the system by the year 2000 (About

18 of the 39 physiographic regions of Canada have yet to contain a park. Canadian park policy requires that at least one park be established within each of the 39 specific regions.)

The expectations are that Canada, as a developed country of the North, has the knowledge, technology, and initiative to be a world leader in the realm of parks and protected areas. The truth of the matter is that Canada has indeed taken a leading role with respect to policy and management of such areas. Comparatively, though, many of the developing countries of the South have been far more conscientious in the development of their parks systems. Panama, Nicaragua and Costa Rica, for example, have set aside much higher percentages of their national territories as parks and protected areas. Despite Canada's low productivity in the establishment of parks, public opinion is in favour of the creation of more wilderness areas. Reid *et al.* (1995) illustrate that on the basis of a survey of over 1,500 residents of British Columbia, respondents, on average, would be willing to pay between $108 and $130 annually in taxes for a doubling of designated wilderness areas, and between $149 and $156 for a tripling of wilderness areas.

Parks have evolved, globally, to be managed according to the ecological and human conditions of the environments that they inhabit. National parks in Britain (England and Wales), for example, are managed from a very different perspective from those in other Western societies. According to Henderson (1992 : 397), conservation in Britain is based on a 'steady state of human intervention designed to maintain a given habitat at a particular successional stage in perpetuity', which he feels is the most unnatural conservation policy possible. British national parks are essentially living, working landscapes, and administratively it is the responsibility of a National Park Authority (which operates within the local government system and whose members are appointed by the government in consultation with the Countryside Commission) to: (1) preserve and enhance park natural beauty; (2) promote access, use, and enjoyment; and (3) ensure proper practices of agriculture, forestry, and economics (Exmoor National Park 1990). The result is that there is a significant amount of socio-economic activity occurring within the 11 national parks of Britain, owing to the fact that virtually none of the land in England or Wales is excluded from human activity (Phillips 1985). Exmoor

National Park, the second smallest park in the system, for example, has a resident population of 10,000 and hosts 2.4 million visitors per year, and is almost 80 per cent privately owned (Exmoor National Park 1990). The park plan goes on to explain the role that major developments, economic development, agriculture and forestry, housing, services and facilities, and tourism play in the context of the park, which is consistent with the types of activities that occur in British parks in general (Phillips 1985). Based on this philosophy of use, tourism therefore has a significant role to play within the national parks and is not questioned to the point that it is in other national parks. However,, the tourism industry is still expected to operate within guidelines established by the Countryside Commission and the English Tourist Board (Countryside Commission 1990).

The national parks of Britain, as suggested above, are somewhat of an anomaly in that they do not meet the category II criteria of the IUCN (International Union for the Conservation of Nature and National Resources) on national parks. Internationally, then, guidelines have been established in an effort to both control and direct countries in how best to set-aside specific lands and water. Phillips (1985) feels that the national parks of Britain would be better classified as protected landscapes, or category V of the IUCN guidelines. (See Table 3.1)

Protected Areas: the International Scene

A number of international agencies have become involved in the process of aiding individual countries in the process of identifying candidate natural areas. As the need for more protected areas continues to gain momentum globally, such agencies have found it necessary to categorise areas relative to the types of land use and practices of conservation found in different countries. Britain, for example, does not have the type of landscape that would enable the British to establish the magnitude of wilderness reserves that are found in Australia.

Table 3.1
Categories for Conservation Management

Category I–Scientific Reserve/Strict Nature Reserve

Areas with some outstanding ecosystem features and/or species of flora and fauna of national scientific importance, representative of particular natural areas, fragile life forms or ecosystems, important biological or geological diversity, or areas of particular importance to the conservation of genetic resources. Concern is for continuance of natural processes and strict control of human interference.

Category II–National Park

A relatively large area where one or several ecosystems are not materially altered by human use, the highest competent government authority has taken steps to prevent or control such alteration, and visitors are allowed to enter, under special conditions for inspirational, educative, cultural and recreative uses.

Category III–Natural Monument/Natural Landmark

Area normally contains one or more specific natural features of outstanding national significance which because of uniqueness or rarity should be protected. Ideally little or no sign of human activity.

Category IV–Nature Conservation Reserve/Managed Nature Reserve/ Wildlife Sanctuary

A variety of areas fall into this category. Although each has as its primary purpose the protection of nature, the production of harvestable renewable resources may play a secondary role in management. Habitat manipulation may be required to provide optimum conditions for species, communities, or features of special interest.

Category V–Protected Landscape or Seascape

A broad category embracing a wide variety of semi-natural and cultural landscapes within various nations. In general, two types of areas, those where landscapes possess special aesthetic qualities resulting from human-land interaction and those that are primarily natural areas managed intensively for recreational and tourist uses.

Category VI–Resource Reserve (Interim Conservation Unit)

Normally extensive, relatively isolated, and lightly inhabited areas under considerable pressure for colonisation and greater exploration. Often not well understood in natural, land use, or cultural terms. Maintenance of existing conditions to allow for studies of potential uses and their effects as a basis for decisions.

Category VII–Natural Biotic Area/Anthropological Reserve

Natural areas where the influence or technology of modern humans has not significantly interfered with or been absorbed by the traditional ways of life of inhabitants. Management is oriented to maintenance of habitat for traditional societies.

Category VIII–Multiple Use Management Area/Managed Resource Area

Large areas suitable for production of wood products, water, pasture, wildlife, marine products and outdoor recreation. May contain nationally unique or exceptional natural features. Planning and management on a sustained-yield basis with protection through zoning or other means for special features or processes.

Category IX–Biosphere Reserve

Intended to conserve representative natural areas throughout the world through creation of global and national networks of reserves. Can include representative natural biomes, or communities, species of unique interest, example of harmonious landscapes resulting from traditional uses, and modified or degraded landscapes capable of restoration to more natural conditions. Biosphere reserves provide benchmarks for monitoring environmental change and areas for science, education and training.

Category X–World Heritage Site

To protect natural—and also cultural—features considered to be of world heritage quality; examples include outstanding illustrations of the major stages of earth's evolutionary history, habitats where populations of rare or endangered species of plants and animals still survive, and also outstanding archaeological or architectural sites. Stress on maintenance of heritage values for worldwide public enlightenment, and to provide for research and environmental monitoring.

Category XI–Wetlands of International Importance (Ramsar)

Marshes, swamps, and other wetlands of value for flood control, nutrient production, wildlife habitat, and related purposes. Management procedures designed to prevent destruction and deterioration through national agreement to an international convention known as Ramsar after the site in Iran where the convention was initially agreed to by a number of founding countries.

Source : Nelson 1991.

The IUCN has been especially effective in charting a course for the planning, establishment, and management of protected areas globally. Its categories for conservation management illustrate the variability of protected areas that have been developed internationally, each of which focuses on different aspects of development (the level of tourism infrastructure and use) and preservation. The extent of the work of the IUCN goes well beyond the categorisation of protected areas, though, to include establishing a system of biogeographical provinces of the world; publishing lists and directories of protected areas; publishing conceptual papers on protected areas; publishing the quarterly journal *Parks;* cooperating with United Nations agencies (e.g. UNESCO); holding international meetings, such as the World Conferences on Parks and Protected Areas; and supporting field projects for the establishment and management of protected areas (Eidsvik 1993 : 280).

In addition to the IUCN, a series of other international organisations have been activated for the purpose of conservation. The World Heritage Convention of 1972 (UNESCO) provides for the establishment of natural and cultural sites of outstanding universal value. Such sites are woven into the fabric of existing protected areas and, although the system does not impose any new management criteria on existing parks, it does impose an element of symbolism and prestige for countries that maintain such site. As of 1994, there were some 350 sites worldwide.

A considerable amount of attention has been paid to biosphere reserves as a means by which to overcome some of the problems related to the use of park environments. The biosphere reserve concept grew out of the 1970 UNESCO general meeting which provided the impetus for the development of the Man and the Biosphere programme meetings, which started the following year, and the first reserves started to appear in 1976. The biosphere reserve concept is founded upon three themes: development, conservation, and research. Spatially, these reserves incorporate three distinct zones: (1) a core area, which is minimally disturbed and strictly protected; (2) a buffer, situated around the core and allowing certain types of resource use that do not disturb the core, and (3) a transition zone, which extends outwards into the adjacent territories with no fixed boundary and allowing a full range of human uses. Seven guidelines define the establishment criteria of biosphere reserves. Biospheres work as a linked network of natural areas; they are representations of the 227 biogeographical provinces; they will be examples of special environments (i.e. natural biomes), large in size to ensure effective conservation; they will act as benchmarks for research, education and training; they will have some form of legal protection; and they will have incorporated within them existing protected areas.

Eidsvik (1983) illustrates that the biosphere is a unique concept relative to other types of protected areas in that it operates under the premise of an inverted pyramid, where the decision-making does not necessarily occur from a centralised federal authority, but rather from the grassroots level with support at various other levels. Eidsvik described this concept as follows :

> The system is designed to support and cherish the participant, operating at his or her own level.... Those services that cannot be provided by individuals or their communities then become the responsibility of local agencies. More specialised services come from the provincial governments—and finally, highly specialised residual services are provided by federal agencies.

In practice there are examples of the success of the biosphere reserve concept in the developed and developing worlds. In Canada, for example, the Long Point Biosphere Reserve and region in Ontario operates in partnership with a variety of municipal, provincial, and federal agencies (Francis 1985) including the Canadian Wildlife Service, Transport Canada, the Ontario Ministry of Natural Resources, the private Long Point Company land, a conservation authority, a regional municipality and other private land holdings, all in an area of approximately 33,000 ha. Similarly, in Mexico, the Sian Ka'an Biosphere Reserve in the Yucatán Peninsula was developed as a result of local efforts to safeguard this 1.3 million acre territory. A non-profit organisation, the Amigos de Sian Ka'an, was established as a result of the initial reserve establishment deliberations, whose responsibility it is to mediate between the private sector and various levels of government. Tourism, owing to the proximity of the reserve to Caucún, has grown significantly in the past twenty years, posing both a threat and an opportunity. Crucial to the viability of the reserve, therefore, is the cooperation between levels of government, the ENGO, and local people, in coming together to solve common dilemmas and improve the quality of their lives. This has prompted the executive director of Amigos de Sian Ka'an to remark that 'If the people who live in the reserve support it, they will take care of it. If not, no amount of guards will stop them' (Norris 1992 : 33). Despite the positives of the biosphere programme, there are those who have suggested that it still exists as a top-down approach to conservation, without the commitment to localism that should exist in such areas (Janzen in Chase 1989).

Ecosystem Management and Protected Areas

As identified previously in Figure 3.1, parks management has evolved significantly over time. One of the finest examples of this evolution is the development of the ecosystem management philosophy, which has blossomed as a consequence of the realisation that in order effectively to safeguard an environment one must scientifically understand the relationships and processes that exist within such a setting. The biodiversity crisis, new ecological theories, and dissatisfaction with governmental regularly measures also contributed to the birth of this mode of thinking (Grumbine 1996). Foremost, biological and social systems theory became the foundation of ecosystem management, once it became clear that ecological sustainability can be attained only through substantial societal change. Indeed, as Francis (n.d.) suggests, we must begin to see ourselves as integral components of complex ecosystems, components in turn related to one another over a variety of spatial and temporal scales. The feeling is that the species with which we share ecosystems have inherent value in and of themselves, and should not be judged on the basis of their ability to provide us with resources, but rather as important elements within the complex system.

In definition, ecosystem management, according to the Canadian Environmental Advisory Council (CEAC), as it relates to its important function in the planning and management of parks and protected areas, refers to the 'integrated management of natural landscapes, ecological processes, wildlife species and human activities both within and adjacent to protected areas' (CEAC 1991 : 38). The following definition, put forward by Johnson and Agee (1988), emphasises the inclusion of both social and ecological processes that help shape and transform ecosystems. Hence, we can never separate human and biophysical elements within an ecosystem; they are inseparable. As a species, we live in or visit just about every inhabitable space on the planet that we can.

> Ecosystem management involves regulating internal ecosystem structure and function, plus inputs and outputs, to achieve socially desirable conditions. It includes, within a chosen and not always static geographic setting, the usual array of planning and management activities but conceptualised in a systems framework; identification of issues through research, public involvement, and political analysis; goal setting; plan development; use allocation; activity development (resources management, interpretation); monitoring; and evaluation. Interagency coordination is often a key element of successful ecosystem management, but is not an end in itself. Success in ecosystem management is

ultimately measured by the goals achieved, not by the amount of coordination. (Johnson and Agee 1988 : 7)

According to Chipeniuk (1988), the management of parks from an ecological perspective is not complete, and ecosystems are not natural, because they lack a principal component of these ecosystems that existed at the time of European contact: human hunters and gatherers who played a role as predators. Chipeniuk argues that this is a niche which, for biological and socio-cultural reasons, must be filled (in Canada and other similar environments around the world) by human surrogates. In a biological sense, the environment would be returned to more of a natural state (i.e. pre-contact); while from the socio-cultural context the return of people as part of the functioning of park ecosystems would cease to delude people about the proper place of human beings in the natural world. This point is touched on by Pretty and Pimbert (1995 : D8), who argue that when people (i.e. local indigenous people) are excluded from conservation the goals of conservation are at risk. They write that 'some "pristine rain forests," assumed to be untouched by human hands, are now known to have once supported thriving agricultural communities. The "pristine" concept of the wilderness is an urban myth that exists only in our imagination'.

The study of the relations between humans and their respective environments, or human ecology (Burch 1988), has been described as a field of research that has potential to institute the human dimensions in ecosystem management along with the bio-physical. In fact, Nelson (1993) describes ecosystem management and human ecology as different sides of the same coin—where human ecologists and biologists should find common ground. Nelson (*ibid.*: 74) has identified five ways in which human ecology can aid in ecosystem management—

(1) by presenting a historical understanding of an area in terms of nature and humans and their interactions;

(2) by doing a history systematically in terms of the culture which defines humans, e.g. policies and institutions, perceptions, attitudes, values, technology;

(3) by presenting the history spatially in terms of similarities and differences over space;

(4) by linking human studies to concepts or ideas that are the concern of other professionals, for example, the concept of landscape, which has roots in architecture, geography, geology and other fields such as biology; and

(5) by presenting historical understanding in terms that are meaningful and attractive to a wide range of citizens; by drawing people to the human-nature interface—to the dynamics of ecosystem management, from a human perspective—to complement those people drawn to it from a biological or scientific perspective.

Peterson (1996 : 27, 28) takes a more hard-hitting approach to linking human ecology and ecosystem management. He advocates four extreme approaches to human ecology that humans use to define their relationship with the planet. These include—

(1) *Dominion*—This implies rule by a monarch, where humans are held to be in charge of the earth. They can be exploitative or serve the well-being of all, in their role as 'king'.

(2) *Stewardship*—This paradigm puts humans in the role of caretaker of the earth, managing the earth in trust as an agent for some employer or client. The client may be the human race or the earth itself.

(3) *Participation*—This role sees humans in symbiosis with other species of the planet, so that a position of equity is conveyed. Humans serve by constructing cooperative and complementary relationships through which all other species are better off.

(4) *Abdication*—Here, all rights to prosper are relinquished when such rights conflict with the functional values of other species. Humans are caught in the predator-prey relationship just as other species are.

The implications of these four approaches to ecosystem management, according to Peterson, are that effective human management of ecosystems will not occur without a clear understanding of the place of people in the context of the ecosystem.

A good example of the application of human ecology principles to parks management is found in the work of Slocombe and Nelson (1992). These authors identify a number of pressures that exist within parks and protected areas as a result of internal (illegal entry, removal of flora and fauna) and external (pollution mining) threats. Their paper examines three protected areas (Kluane National Park in Canada; Wrangell-St Elias National Park and Preserve in the United States; and Kakadu National Park in Australia) in developing management responses to issues within these areas. Eight management criteria termed dimensions of difference, were developed to assess and compare the parks, namely access, tourism, resource extraction, aboriginals' role, administration issues, scientific research, interpretation and regional integration. Slocombe and Nelson conclude that interest is growing in human ecological approaches to parks and protected areas, as they apply to many regions around the world.

Although human ecology is a well-established discipline, its place in tourism studies has not been well represented. For example, in a recent review of the journal *Human Ecology,* I found just two examples of human ecology and tourism. Both papers explored the resource competition that exists between recreational anglers and local users of the resource base. Berkes (1984) discovered that although no ecological competition existed between local and non-local people, a type of perceptual competition existed between the two. Conversely, de Castro and Bergossi (1996) found that competition existed between tourists and locals over certain fish species, but only at certain times of the year. In an effort to better link tourism studies and human ecology, Fennell and Butler have recently developed a human ecological approach to tourism group interactions by suggesting that various forms of tourism (e.g. ecotourism, general interest tourism) share specific relationships (predatory, competitory, neutral and symbiotic) with each other, local people, other land users, and the tourism industry, all within the context of a network of land, including parks and protected areas, town sites, and other settings. The paper explores the notion that each of the various stakeholders identify in a tourism setting value and use resources differently and therefore place different levels of pressure on each other and the resource base.

CONCLUSION

The philosophical issues related to the place and role of humans in the environment have been explored most effectively through conservation and preservation. Parks as manifestations of the development of conservation must continue to act as test sites for human–environment interactions. We must continue to employ new strategies to enable people to strike a fair and equitable balance between use and preservation in a world that perpetuates the value of human beings at the expense of other life forms, and which continually encroaches upon the earth's most sensitive and significant regions, through tourism and other land uses. The principles put forward in ecosystem management and human ecology may help us to better understand the place of humans in the natural world. However, this technical and scientific information must be analysed in the context of appropriate philosophical and conceptual questions which we have been asking, as evident in the writings of many of the Romantic scholars, for some time.

4

Professionalism in Tourism

The discussion that follows is designed to act as a continuation of some of the many issues dealt with in the previous chapter (i.e. regulation and planning). For example, Buckley and Pannell (1990) write that environmental impacts might be minimised through the use of a combination of factors including planning and regulation, incentives to encourage or discourage particular activities, hardening of sites receiving high levels of use, and through the use of education both on- and off-site. Such policy-related actions are increasingly required, according to Goodwin (1995), to ensure that tourism development is consistent with the needs of both local people and the environment. Tourism and ecotourism policy encompasses a broad spectrum of concerns related to the implementation of tourism programmes around the world, including social, ecological and economic relationships; but also how tourism affects or is affected by tourists, local people, operators, government, and so on. In addition, much discussion has surrounded the notion of regulation as a means by which to provide a stronger element of control in how ecotourism products are shaped and implemented. Regulation, therefore, is also an integral part of this chapter. The final part of the chapter deals with certification and accreditation in the ecotourism industry. It is suggested that the industry is committing itself further to these programmes as a means by which to offer a higher standard of quality and professionalism in the field.

Tourism Policy

In a simplistic sense, tourism policy is the identification of a series of goals and objectives which help an agency—usually a governmental one—in the process of planning the tourism industry. According to Akehurst (1992), however, policy development is much more detailed. It is further defined as :

> a strategy for the development of the tourism sector. . .that establishes objectives and guidelines as a basis for what needs to be done. This means identifying and agreeing objectives; establishing priorities; placing in a Community context the roles of national governments, national tourist organisations, local governments and private-sector businesses; establishing possible co-ordination and implementation of agreed programmes to solve identified problems, with monitoring and evaluation of these programmes. (Akehurst 1992 : 217)

In this sense it is the coordination of many organisations and agencies involved in the provision of tourism services, and the planning, development and management of these groups.

It is felt that all countries should endeavour to create tourism policy to guide their planning, management and development of tourism consistently throughout a region and as a means by which to use resources in a wise and efficient manner (Jenkins 1991). The sector most responsible for the impetus to create policy is government, in either a passive (e.g. legislation is introduced but is not intended to discriminate in favour of the tourism industry) or an active manner, where government takes action to discriminate in favour of the tourism sector managerially (through the creation of objectives and legislative support) and/or developmentally (in the establishment and operation of tourism facilities). In a similar context Lickorish (1991) suggests that governments have given low priority to the establishment of policy in tourism, particularly in the developed world (the first policy reports were established by the European Community in 1986). The reason for this is that governments have traditionally viewed tourism development as lying within the realm of the private sector (Lickorish 1991; Pearce 1989). If centralised action has not been taken within a country, often regions or localities have taken responsibility but, according to Lickorish, with uneven results. In addition, policy-related problems are compounded by the fact that government policies related to tourism and the environment can be quite divergent. Ministries of agriculture, the environment, tourism and industry, and transport may all vary in their approach to environmental policy.

Coccossis (1996) feels that there has not been a good understanding between the complex nature of the environment and tourism (e.g. the synergistic effects of tourism), coupled with a high degree of administrative fragmentation. In addition, he writes that environmental conservation was perceived as a threat to social and economic development, a threat which has only recently subsided as a result of our efforts towards the clarification of sustainable development. Without due regard to appropriate development guidelines, the integrity of public and private lands within communities has often been at risk owing to the sacrificing of socioecological values at the expense of profit. A key point in Coccossis's argument is that environmental policies now are characterised by a more holistic, ecosystem based approach that relies less on specific issues and more on a regional integrated perspective. This wider approach involves the following—

(1) linking development policy with environmental management. As a first step, the review of projects, plans and programmes from an environmental point of view should be instituted;

(2) regional-level environmental management schemes which would provide a framework for guiding local environmental management programmes;

(3) integration of tourism development and environmental management policies at the local regional, and national level; and

(4) increasing local capacity to cope with environmental issues, particularly in rapidly developing tourist destination areas.

Priority areas identified by Coccossis (1996) in Europe for sustainable tourism development, utilising the aforementioned concepts, include coastal areas, rural areas, built environment and urban areas, and islands. One of the best examples of policy related to hotel development was the implementation of measures to control the height of hotel development in Bali, Indonesia, and other places around the world in the 1980s. Hotels could not be built higher than the tallest palm trees to avoid the unsightly nature of these developments. Hence, the development would fit into the landscape rather than dominate it.

In support of what Coccossis illustrates above. Fayos-Sola (1996) writes that tourism policy has started to change in line with the evolving nature of the tourism industry. Consistent with the paradigmatic shift in the 1980s away from mass tourism to alternative forms of tourism, the industry has given way to globalisation of markets, supersegmentation, new technologies, and an increased sense of social and ecological responsibility. Competitiveness is a key function of the tourism industry and it is based on quality and efficiency rather than the quantity, which has been the *modus operandi* of mass tourism. Conversely, tourism policy objectives have undergone three distinct generations, according to Fayos-Sola (1996). The first generation was based on large numbers of visitors, the maximisation of revenues from tourism, and the creation of numbers of jobs, indicative of the mass tourism paradigm. The second generation evolved from the economic difficulties of the 1970s, including growth-recession fluctuations. In this stage, social, economic and ecological impacts are better understood, while the economic and legal objectives are redefined in tourism's contribution to societal well-being. The final generation shows competitiveness as a key function of the vitality of the tourism industry. In addition, both total quality management and the partnership between public, private, and not-for-profit agencies is underscored, leading to a more symbiotic relationship between sectors. As such, the politics of policy-making for the twenty-first century will go beyond the conventional discussions related to marketing, promotion, tax incentives, accommodation, and transportation to more holistic centred issues related to the environment, social impacts, issues of rational and equitable access (who gets what, when and how), and the international regulation of health and safety issues (Richter 1991). Richter further illustrates that the political interest in policy is coming of age and that the democratisation of the electorate may prove to be formidable proponents in shaping key tourism decisions.

In a different line of thinking from the policy issues outlined above, Hjalager (1996a) argues that innovation must be the key to future policies and regulation designed to limit tourism's impact on the resource base. She feels that policy, when it is considered, is hampered first by the fact that it is governed by ideology and personal sympathies rather than the need for balance, and second by the fact that cost is unlikely to be considered in implementation. Her research touches on three policy control mechanisms: the market, bureaucracies, and clans (industry in cooperation with other stakeholders). For example, Hjalager writes that bureaucracies regulate tourism in basically two fashions: (1) by directing tourists, locals and the industry through legislation, and (2) through the provision of tourism infrastructure. (see Table 4.1) Central to Hjalager's thesis is the notion that regions must be open to alternative modes of regulation in addressing significant and challenging environmental issues.

CASE STUDY 4.1

The Regulation of Whalewatching in Canada

The impact of ecotourism on the beluga whale population of the St Lawrence River, Canada, has prompted Blane and Jackson (1994) to call for stricter policies in the control of such vessels. The authors found that the high number of trips/vessels in the area of the whales was affecting their behaviour. They recommended that the number of operators should be restricted, that low speed limits should be spatially increased and enforced, and that boats should be required to travel around beluga pods in an appropriate fashion. Further, the authors suggested that policing should be accomplished by the Canadian government and informally by peers (i.e. operators). Such regulations have been addressed on the west coast of Canada by whalewatching operators, government, and other interested groups, and a set of guidelines for the industry to follow has been developed. A recent draft of a document by Whale Watching Operators North West advocates the following: (1) stay approximately 100 metres away form the whales; (2) operators should be familiar with the Canadian Federal Fisheries Act; (3) slow down half a mile before arriving at the whales; (4) whales should be approached slowly at any time; (5) when approaching whales from the front, STOP and allow whales to come to you; (6) when approaching from behind, move to the outside of the nearest whales or boats, parallel to the direction of travel at a similar or slower speed; (7) when travelling with the whales, do not alter speed or change course abruptly; (8) never make high-speed runs through the middle of a group of whales or boats; (9) avoid approaching whales that are feeding; (10) try to work with the whales in rotation; and (11) do not reposition your vessel by the leap-frog method.

Table 4.1
Innovation's Place in Tourism Policy and Regulation

Instruments	*How the environmental effect is achieved*	*Influence on Innovation*
Emission standards. Inspection in order to control	Industrial 'end of pipe' norms expressed according to carrying capacities. Development per-missions with environmental standards	Control may raise standards, severe control may lead to the development of new techniques. No evidence that tourism will take the innovation lead.
Compulsory use of specific energy resources or specific technologies (e.g. district heating or waste treatment systems)	Obtaining economies of scale in environmental management systems.	Typically, innovation will not take place in tourist industries, but with specialised plants and suppliers.
Zoning in order to limit or control opportunities for development. Control of land use.	Limiting the developer's activities according to carrying capacities or environmental objectives.	Probably none.
Zoning of tourists' access to vulnerable resources or areas.	Visitor control systems and regulation of tourism by volumes. Compulsory methods or training, motivation.	Opportunities for development of IT instrument combined with communication/interpretation instruments.

Source : Hjalager 1996a.

Ecotourism and Policy

In many countries, ecotourism is presently at the policy consideration and initiation stage, with the recognition that further political and socio-economic coordination must exist for it to proceed. Policy development has only started to be initiated as a result of the lack of consensus as to what constitutes appropriate ecotourism development and activities. This has been the case in Hawaii, as identified by the Center for Tourism Policy Studies (1994). This group has identified a number of policy recommendations to address in developing Hawaii's ecotourism industry, including: (1) a state ecotourism policy and ecotourism development plan; (2) inter-agency coordination and cooperation with the private sector; (3) increased funding support through direct and indirect means; and (4) active community participation in planning and decision-making. These recommendations are further broken down into integrated planning, public- and private-sector roles, research, land use, conservation, preservation, funding, marketing, operator concerns, socio-cultural concerns, regulation, monitoring, and education and training. As a prime US destination, Hawaii is realising that apart from its extensive mass tourism industry, there is a definite market for ecotourists based on interests in whalewatching and the rainforest. Although rough estimates indicate that ecotourism represents about 5 per cent of Hawaiian tourism revenue, there is the feeling that ecotourism is on the rise in this state (Marinelli (1997), which is good news given the negligible tourism growth in Hawaii over the past decade.

Much like the Center for Tourism Policy Studies cited above, Liu (1994) suggests that government policy is one of the keys to supporting the development of ecotourism. Her work on behalf of the American Affiliated Pacific Islands discusses the importance of government policy as a means by which to regulate and monitor the industry in a way that balances protection and restriction without hindering the individual operator. This means a balance between development and conservation, supply *versus* demand, benefits *versus* costs, and people *versus* the environment. In addition. Liu feels that government must play a leadership role in providing the necessary financing, management skills, and knowledge so the private sector can operate smoothly and efficiently. This means government must (Liu 1994 : 8, 9) :

(1) facilitate efficient private-sector activity by minimising market interference and relying on competition as a means of control;

(2) ensure a sound macro-economic environment;

(3) guarantee law and order, and the just settlement of disputes;

(4) ensure the provision of appropriate infrastructures;

(5) ensure the development of human resources;

(6) protect the public interest without obstructing private-sector activity with too many regulations;

(7) promote private sector activity by not competing in the business arena with private enterprise; and

(8) acknowledge the role of small business entrepreneurs and facilitate their activities.

Liu (1994) has developed a public-sector guide for the implementation of ecotourism, as set out in Table 4.2. These are the points that should be considered for the purpose of implementing appropriate ecotourism policy.

Table 4.2
Policy Implementation Framework

Development objectives—Establish economic, ecological and socio-cultural objectives in consultation with local communities; designate specific areas for ecotourism development.

Inventories—Survey and analyse the region's ecology, history, culture, economy, resources, land use, and tenure; inventory and evaluate existing and potential ecotourist attractions, activities, accommodation, facilities, and transportation; construct or consolidate development policies and plans, especially tourism master plans.

Infrastructure and facilities—Provide the appropriate infrastructure and facilities, avoiding a reliance on foreign capital; establish means to assist the private sector in developing ecotourism enterprises in line with ecological and cultural standards.

Market—Analyse present and future domestic and international ecotourism markets and establish marketing goals; known and understand the market in achieving goals; assist the private sector in its development of marketing strategies.

Carrying capacity—Strive to understand the social and ecological limits of use of an area through appropriate management and research;

establish social and ecological indicators of use and impact; implement an appropriate pre-formed planning and management framework.

Development—Establish a development policy giving consideration to balanced economic, ecological, and social factors; form a development plan on the basis of attractions, transportation, and ecotourism regions; assist developers to plan and build ecologically.

Economic—Consider ways to enhance economic benefits; conduct present and future economic analyses; ensure that profits are made, locals benefit, and public revenues are self-sustaining.

Environment—Consistently evaluate the impact of ecotourism on the resource base; link ecotourism with other resource conservation measures (e.g. parks and protected areas).

Culture—Evaluate the socio-cultural impact of ecotourism, prevent negative impacts, and reinforce positive outcomes; empower local people to become decision-makers; conduct a social audit of social impacts.

Standards—Apply development and design standards to facilities and accommodation; facilitate the adherence to standards by providing financial or tax incentives and access to specialists.

Human resources—Promote job creation and entrepreneurship; establish community awareness programmes; provide adequate education and training for local people.

Organisation—Establish a working relationship between public, private and not-for-profit organisations.

Regulations and monitoring—Establish legislation/regulations to promote ecotourism development, through support for tourism organisations, tour operators, accommodation; establish facility standards.

Data system and implementation—Establish an integrated ecotourism data system for continuous operation that provides research and marketing information; identify ecotourism implementation techniques; and collaborate with private industry and educational institutions in implementation.

Source : Liu 1994.

Increasingly, planners and developers are realising that policy must involve the many stakeholders who stand to be impacted by ecotourism development, as suggested at the outset of this chapter. According to Ceballos-Lascuráin (1996a: 85-91), some of these groups include protected-area personnel, local communities, the tourism industry, NGOs, financial institutions, consumers and national ecotourism councils. One of the finest examples of policy development involving stakeholder involvement in ecotourism can be found in the Australian National Ecotourism Strategy (Commonwealth Department of Tourism 1994). In this document an integrated approach to the development of ecotourism has been adopted with the belief that development and management of Ecotourism is fundamental to optimising the benefits it offers. This strategy is truly a national document in that it integrates the collective opinions of Australians through the implementation of a series of public consultation workshops involving government, industry, conservation groups, educational institutions and community groups. (The stakeholder approach used in this strategy has been outlined by Boo (1992), who suggests that there are several stakeholder groups that must be involved in the development of ecotourism initiatives). The intent of the strategy is summarised as follows: 'to provide broad direction for the future of ecotourism by identifying priority issues for its sustainable development and recommending approaches for addressing these issues' (Commonwealth Department of Tourism 1994 : 6). The bulk of the strategy concentrates on a variety of issues, objectives and actions which are essentially steps towards putting policy and planning initiatives into practice. The 12 objectives of the strategy are set out in Table 4.3.

It is the ultimate aim of these directives to move Australia to create an ecologically and culturally sustainable ecotourism industry in line with the ideals of sustainable development. The development of this document was instrumental in demonstrating to the rest of the world the advanced state of ecotourism in Australia, and it is a model which other governments can follow. For example, the Ecotourism Task Force in association with Tourism Saskatchewan (the government–private industry consortium that leads tourism development in this Canadian province) has developed a similar document which will be the basis of the ecotourism industry for the future. Recommendations (among others) include the development of an accreditation process, the development of cooperative relationships with other land-users, and the construction of sustainable ecolodge facilities using state-of-the-art technologies and modelling.

As regions and countries make the decision to plan and develop an ecotourism industry, Ceballos-Lascuráin (1996a) advocates following a basic planning process such as the one identified below. Policy may naturally evolve out of first identifying many of the

Table 4.3
Australian National Ecotourism Strategy Objectives

Strategy component	*Objective*
Ecological sustainability	Facilitate the application of ecologically sustainable principles and practices across the tourism industry.
Integrated regional planning	Develop a strategic approach to integrated regional planning based on ecologically sustainable principles and practices and incorporating ecotourism.
Natural resource management	Encourage a complementary and compatible approach between ecotourism activities and conservation in natural resource management.
Regulation	Encourage industry self-regulation of ecotourism through the development and implementation of appropriate industry standards and accreditation.
Infrastructure	Where appropriate, support the design and use of carefully sited and constructed infrastructure to minimise visitor impacts on natural resources and to provide for environmental education consistent with bioregional planning objectives.
Impact monitoring	Undertake further study of the impacts of ecotourism to improve the information base for planning and decision-making.
Marketing	Encourage and promote the ethical delivery of ecotourism products to meet visitor expectations and match levels of supply and demand.
Industry standards/accreditation	Facilitate the establishment of high-quality industry standards and a national accreditation system for ecotourism.
Education	Improve the level and delivery of ecotourism education for all target groups.
Involve indigenous people	Enhance opportunities for self-determination, self-management and economic self-sufficiency in ecotourism for Aboriginals.
Viability	Examine the business needs or operators and develop ways in which viability can be improved, either individually or through collective ventures.
Equity considerations	Seek to ensure that opportunities for access to ecotourism experiences are equitable and that ecotourism activities benefit host communities and contribute to natural resource management and conservation.

Source : Commonwealth Department of Tourism, 1994.

catalysts and constraints to the development of the industry. In the case of ecotourism, this process must proceed out of government's general development policy and strategy (if such a strategy exists).

(1) *Study preparation*—Includes the assessment of the type of planning required and the preparation of terms of reference.

(2) *Determination of objectives*—Such objectives must reflect the national or regional government's general ecotourism policy/strategy, and include development priorities, temporal considerations, heritage, marketing and annual growth.

(3) *Survey*—A complete evaluation and inventory of existing resources must be made, especially related to the attraction base. The ultimate aim of this inventory is to link attractions to various market segments and forms of development.

(4) *Analysis and synthesis*—This step involves study in the historical background of tourism in the region, analysing constraints to development, legal and risk management considerations, financing, tax incentives, protection of cultural and natural features, and other economic-related variables (e.g. contribution to GNP, and complementarity with other sectors of the economy).

(5) *Policy and plan formulation*—From an analysis of the synthesis, policies must be structured to reflect the economic, social and ecological needs of the region. Alternative policies should be developed to assess how each fits with the country's overall development policy, from which final policies are derived in the areas of: infrastructure, human resources, transportation, intersectoral coordination, establishment of councils and committees, tax incentives and subsidies, and the creation of tourism programmes.

(6) *Recommendations*—The result is a plan that indicates attractions, tourism development areas, transportation linkages, tour routes, and design and facility standards. Also, recommendations are made for implementation, zoning, land use plans for the future, economic benefits,

education and training, ecological and social impacts, private industry incentives and legislation.

(7) *Implementation and monitoring*—Prior to implementation, the policies and overall plan should be reviewed and ratified legally. Formal review periods should be established and committees or corporations should be developed to help implement or guide the implementation of the various developments.

The prime mandate of many state and provincial tourism authorities is to bolster tourism and ecotourism in their various regions, through the development of new product strategies to capture a larger travel market. Given the marketing premise under which many of these regional bodies operate (they are designed primarily to generate profits through marketing and incentives), the social and ecological elements associated with sustainable tourism and ecotourism often take a back seat. However, with increasing frequency subcommittees are being created within these agencies to deal specifically with ectourism and sustainable development. For example, in 1990 the California Legislature's Senate Select Committee on Tourism and Aviation convened to address the many problems facing the California tourist industry, including energy shortages, the inhospitality of cities, and development overkill in resorts. From this committee's study of these and other dysfunctions, it was suggested that a strong ecotourism ethic be created that could be advantageous economically, socially, and ecologically, for the purpose of generating more positive tourism experiences in the state. In part because of some of these early examples of policy development at the regional level, in 1997. I sent out an E-mail to all North American provincial and state governments requesting information on ecotourism policy and accreditation (over 60 offices). Although the response was rather limited, the overwhelming consensus among regional bodies was that policy and accreditation are 'on the table', meaning that while they have been thought about, little has been done in the way of legislation.

In some cases regions are in the process of stating recommendations to government on how to proceed in the ecotourism sector. For example, Florida recently developed a report, based on the deliberations of an advisory committee, on how to protect and plan for its heritage and commercial assets

(Ecotourism/Heritage Tourism Advisory Committee 1997), with the mission of developing 'a blueprint that identifies goals, strategies and recommendations needed to create a statewide, regionally based plan to effectively protect and promote the natural, coastal, historical, and cultural assets of Florida, and to link these to commercial tourism in Florida'. The plan focuses on forming strategic relationships with agencies in the community, developing inventories of sites, protection of the environment, education and marketing.

Regulation

According to Metelka (1990), regulation refers to the efforts of an agency (government, international or trade) that has been given the authority to regulate the actions of businesses which fall within its jurisdiction. Historically, this has meant that government has seen fit to dictate the actions of, for example, the airline industry in terms of appropriate policies related to safety. The fear, as always, is that if left unchecked, tourism will contribute to a diverse range of social and ecological impacts. More recently, though, the influence of alternative and sustainable forms of tourism has rekindled discussions related to the need to ensure that service and the provision of tourism products stem from appropriate business practices.

The belief that the tourism industry can operate without due regard to its short and long, and direct and indirect impacts is being challenged as more and more there is the recognition that business must be held accountable for its actions. Goodall (1994) provides an excellent overview of regulation through the process of environmental auditing in the context of the British tourism industry. Citing the European Commission, Goodall writes that environmental auditing is essentially a management tool designed to evaluate how well organisations (their management and equipment) are performing towards the safeguarding of the environment through various environmental practices and policies. Goodall (1994) suggests that this environmental tool has technical (e.g. noise reduction technology), legislative (e.g. the 'polluter pays' principle), and business (e.g. the costs and benefits associated with the will to undertake environmental audits) dimensions, which act as both catalysts and constraints to their implementation. In Britain, Goodall writes, environmental auditing is voluntary and thus the responsibility lies within the

Table 4.4
Summary of Policy and Environmental Audit Objectives

Environmental policy objectives for firms	*Key aims of an environmental audit*
1. Compliance with relevant environmental legislation and indication of a willingness to develop reasonable and workable regulations.	1. To judge whether the tourism firm's environmental management system is performing satisfactorily.
2. Reduction or elimination of any negative environmental impacts of current activities and avoidance of any negative impacts from proposed developments.	2. To verify compliance with relevant environmental legislation.
3. Development of environmentally friendly products.	3. To verify compliance with the firm's stated policy.
4. Sustainable use of resources which include increasing efficiency of resource use, minimising waste, the use of environmentally benign inputs and equipment, and the safe disposal of wastes.	4. To minimise human exposure to risk from the environment and to ensure appropriate health and safety provision.
5. The fostering among employees, and also customers and communities in which the firm functions, an understanding of environmental issues.	5. To identify and assess the firm's risk resulting from environmental failure of its activities.
	6. To assess the impact on the environment, both local and global, of its plant, processes and products.
	7. To advise the firm on any environmental improvements it could make.
	8. To review the firm's internal procedures to help it to achieve its environmental objectives.

Source : Goodall (1994).

agency, hence it is not likely to happen owing to the competitive, fragmented, small-scale nature of the industry. Consequently, few tourism agencies have formal environmental policies and management system, and 'Unless required to by law, such firms will only adopt best environmental practice here there is an incontrovertible commercial advantage' (*ibid.*: 663). In summary, Table 4.4 outlines environmental policy and environmental auditing considerations, as suggested by Goodall (*ibid.*: 658).

In reference to the UK outgoing tourism industry Forsyth (1995) discusses the link between sustainability and regulation. His findings suggest that tourism businesses would be in favour of sustainability; however, he feels that because of the fragmented nature of the industry itself (i.e. hotels, tour operators, travel agents, carriers, associations), different industry sectors have separate aims and varied levels of power, and therefore may be unable to implement all forms of sustainable tourism consistently. Another main conclusion of his study was that host governments should be involved in the business of sustainable tourism (through regulation), not necessarily tourism businesses. The implication is that business practice occurs under the umbrella of regional and/or national policy schemes. The problem with such an approach is that such policies would probably be flexible to accommodate demand of the domestic tourism product and flexible in terms of accommodating multinational interest in the destination, which is usually driven by a profit motive.

One of the significant issues related to the imposition of regulatory measures for ecotourism operators is the perceived loss of control in the delivery of services and decision-making. In a discussion of the adventure and ecotourism industry in South Carolina, Tibbetts (1995-96) illustrates that many of the operators in this region favour self-regulation and voluntary guidelines. There is a strong belief by such operators that since they are the ones out there working in the environment, they known how to manage their affairs without government help, how to solve their own problems, and how to take the lead in terms of planning and implementing an appropriate product. This may very well be true, but there are other, more broadly based concerns that may need to be considered. The operation of an ecotourism business involves an interaction with other tourism businesses, other land-users, local people, tourists, and so on. The result is that the potential conflicts that may arise from these interactions (e.g. the overuse of trail systems, and the dumping of wastes in the Galápagos Islands) are not simply local and operator-specific, but rather have larger regional and socio-ecological implications. A key question to address is whether or not policy-makers can afford to provide the time for operators to distil out problems of complementarity and conflict, especially when it is the resource base that should be protected first over the needs of tourists and private industry. We must consider that today, more than ever, businesses must be accountable to themselves, but, more importantly, to society. Given this axiom, it is appropriate that we continue to press the issue of whether or not the tourism industry and environment might better be served by regulation or self-regulation, or indeed both. (see the Australian accreditation process to follow). In addition, research needs to concentrate on the difference and/or similarities between ecotourism and more conventional forms of tourism with respect to regulation and self-regulation, in an attempt to discern whether ecotourism businesses are in fact more ecologically minded than mass tourism firms.

Certification, Accreditation and Professionalism

Along with regulation (as outlined above), there has been an increased focus on the relevance of certification, accreditation and professionalism in the tourism industry over the past few years. Certification and accreditation programmes act as the basis for the education and the provision of skills of those working in the industry. The heightened level of attention afforded to certification and accreditation is discussed by Morrison *et al.* (1992), who identify a number of existing programmes in North America, including programmes for the posts of Certified Travel Counsellor, Certified Hotel Administrator (the two longest-standing programmes), Certified Tour Professional, Certified Meeting Professional, Certified Hotel Sales Executive, Certified Festival Executive, Certified Incentive Travel Executive, Certified Travel Marketing Executive and Certified Exhibit Manager. According to Morrison *et al.* (1992), the two terms 'certification' and 'accreditation' may be differentiated on the following basis—

- *Certification*—A process by which an individual is tested and evaluated in order to determine his or her mastery of a specific body of knowledge, or some portion of a body of knowledge.

- *Accreditation*—A process by which an association or agency evaluates and recognises a programme of study or an institution as meeting certain predetermined standards or qualifications. It applies only to institutions and their programmes of study or their services.

As Morrison *et al.* (1992) point out, certification deals with the individual professional, while accreditation is concerned with programmes and institutions. An interesting conclusion of their research is that certification programmes have grown to replace the university as a means by which to gain expertise and professionalism in the tourism industry. They caution, however, that although certification will indeed increase in the future, it should not be a substitute for travel and tourism degrees. In addition, whereas universities are able to offer a good grounding in the theoretical aspects of tourism, they may also diversify into offering certification options to their graduates through their programme offerings. Outside tourism, the relevance of accreditation has been debated in several other disciplines. Scalet and Adelman (1995), for example, discuss the pros and cons of accreditation in fisheries and wildlife programmes, while Silverman (1992) examines accreditation of undergraduate programmes in environmental health science.

In the realm of adventure recreation, there has been significant debate on how best to certify certain aspects of the adventure programme experience, including standards of programme quality, professional behaviour, professional conduct and risk management (Gass and Williamson 1995). Similarly, these have revolved around the certification of leaders and guides through organisations such as the American Mountain Guides Association and the Wilderness Education Association, while the American Camping Association and the National Recreation and Parks Association have implemented accreditation programmes to meet their own specific needs. Two studies found overwhelming support for accreditation over individual certification as it (accreditation) provided an umbrella to ensure a higher degree of professional credibility and less reliance on individual operators (see Cockrell and Detzel 1985; and Bassin *et al.* 1992). These findings were considered in the recent development of a US national accreditation process that focuses on programming in the adventure recreation field by the AEE (Association for Experiential Education 1993), which is designed to consider the technical (hard) skills of adventure recreation, but also the teaching and ethical elements that need to be consistent from the programme side of the experience. This document provides a means by which to systematically evaluate operations in areas related to ethics, risk management, staff qualifications, transportation and technical skills. For example, with respect to the environmental aspects of river rafting, code 43.B.01 suggests that 'Staff are familiar with the operating sites for rafting. *Explanation:* A pre-site investigation is conducted to understand the conditions as well as the education/therapeutic possibilities. This includes locating appropriate take-out areas and access to safe transportation sites' (AEE 1993 : 82).

According to Gass and Williamson (1995 : 25), this national programme maintains the following accreditation procedure—

(1) *Self-assessment and documentation stage*—Operators must compare their programme against the AEE programme guidelines.

(2) *Verification stage*—A team of between two and four reviewers visit the operator and conduct interviews, inspect equipment, and observe activities as necessary. A standards report card is used to determine whether a component of the programme 'passes', 'fails', is 'conditional' based on the need to remedy the situation, or 'does not apply' in the case where an activity is not associated with a programme.

(3) *Follow-up stage*—Findings from the verification stage are forwarded to the Programme Accreditation Services Committee, who send a recommendation to the AEE Executive Board, who in turn decide whether the programme should receive accreditation.

In further support for the idea of accreditation, Gass and Williamson (1995 : 23) offer the following—

(1) Accreditation provides adventure programmes with the ability to achieve standards without losing the flexibility to decide and design how these standards are met.

(2) Accreditation takes a 'systematic view' of the process of adventure programming rather than dividing it into individualised categories.

(3) Accreditation encourages ongoing improvement through internal and external review.

(4) Accreditation assures clients, agencies and resource managers that a programme has clearly defined and appropriate objectives and maintains conditions under which their achievement can be met reasonably.

As suggested in Chapter 2, ecotourism shares some aspects of adventure recreation/tourism, more from the context of setting than in programming. This element of setting (e.g. tropical rainforests) may provide a component of risk that is absent from other, more conventional forms of tourism. To a lesser extent than adventure travel, ecotourism may be seen as bridging a gap between various forms of adventure recreation and tourism. In comparison to outdoor recreation, however—in particular, outdoor guides and leaders—tourism lags far behind, and as in adventure recreation, programming in ecotourism will be a key issue in the future.

Recently the topic of accreditation and certification has been debated in ecotourism, consistent with this trend in the adventure pursuits industry. For example, Wearing (1995 : 34) suggests that professionalisation and accreditation in ecotourism will continue to be at the forefront of discussions related to regulation and control, as a means by which to provide focus to an industry that is almost impossible to limit (in terms of expansion). He feels that accreditation affords the opportunity to improve tourism industry standards while at the same time ensuring high-quality services and programmes in a very competitive marketplace. Wearing identifies a series of advantages and disadvantages of accreditation as they relate to ecotourism, as follows—

Advantages of Accreditation

(1) The ecotourist has the knowledge of what will be taught, and the approaches used will be the best and the safest.

(2) The ecotour operator has a recognised and accepted methodology and thus increased social status.

(3) The employer of ecotourism guides has knowledge of an accepted industry standard.

(4) The government has the knowledge that new operators have been taught to a minimum standard.

Disadvantages of Accreditation

(1) The idea that one needs a service which is best provided by an expert creates a relationship of mutual dependency and creates a social distance between the ecotourist, the operator, the host community, and the natural environment.

(2) Ecotour operators are assessed on their accomplishments rather than their human characteristics to the effect of depersonalising the human—natural environment relationship.

(3) Professionals can tend to rationalise and focus on facts, objective data, and procedures, thus potentially losing the intrinsic, intuitive association so often formed through ecotourism.

(4) Through commodification, the operator may come to view the natural and cultural environments as a means to an end and so become alienated from the natural world and hence unable to encourage the ecotourist or encourage environmental awareness.

(5) Loss of perceived freedom by the individual ecotourist, who feels he or she must do as the operator says; this restricts the ecotourism experience.

(6) The imposed structure that is required to assess or measure the ecotour operator entails limitations.

The message put forward by Wearing is that although accreditation would certainly reduce risk, increase standards, and increase status, there is a danger of restricting innovation and accessibility within the ecotourism industry. One of the significant dilemmas, therefore is the degree to which the industry can afford to emphasise innovation and accessibility at the expense of ensuring that proper standards are being upheld. The issue is one that clearly requires more time and education to be provided for operators in the field. In addition, it is a normative concern as the likelihood for compliance is directly related to how operators feel individually, but also collectively, about the process of accreditation. If it is imposed upon them, only time will tell how operators will react to the imposition. However, in time accreditation may be fully accepted as proper or appropriate business practice.

A good example of the accreditation process in action can be found in Australia, where those working in the field, i.e. operators, submit to a standardised procedure. At present, operators are given a core level of accreditation if they satisfy the programme's basic criteria; however, the system encourages operators to implement measures beyond the standards of the core criteria in earning advanced standing. Eligibility for accreditation is based on eight criteria (Chester 1997 : 9). According to these criteria, ecotourism—

(1) focuses on personally experiencing natural areas in ways that lead to greater understanding and appreciation;

(2) integrates into each experience opportunities to understand natural areas;

(3) represents best practice for ecologically sustainable tourism;

(4) productively contributes to the conservation of natural areas;

(5) provides constructive, ongoing contributions to local communities;

(6) interprets, involves, and is sensitive to different cultures (particularly indigenous ones);

(7) consistently meets client expectations; and

(8) its marketing is accurate and leads to realistic expectations.

In Australia there was resounding support for the idea of ecotourism accreditation in the mid-1990s (McArthur 1997) which culminated in the launching of the National Ecotourism Accreditation Programme at Australia's 1996 national meeting (refer to the earlier part of the chapter for a discussion of the strategy). Accreditation is offered to those operators working in the accommodation, tour operations, and attractions sectors, and operators are accredited by first completing an application (through a nomination process involving three referees), and by paying a one-off application fee and an annual fee. Table 4.5 provides an overview of this fee structure.

Table 4.5
Ecotourism Accreditation Fees in Aus $ (from November 14, 1996)

Fees-based on annual business turnover ($)	*0-100,000 turnover p.a.*	*100,00–250,000*	*250,000–1,000,000*	*1,000,000–-3,000,000*	*3,000,000–and over*
Ecotourism accreditation document fee (per. doc):					
Members	75	75	75	75	75
Non-members	175	175	175	175	175
Application fee (only in year 1)	75	100	175	250	400
Annual renewal fee	100	150	300	500	750
Total fee in year 1:					
Members	250	325	550	825	1225
Non-members	350	425	650	925	1325

Source : McArthur 1997.

One of the key features of the Australian accreditation initiative is the level and style of enforcement employed in the programme. Each of the applicants is monitored in four ways: (1) the applicant's honesty in completing application documents; (2) feedback from clients; (3) feedback from referees (random selection of operators); and (4) through random audits.

Professionalism

A typical end-product of the acceditation and certification debate in the tourism industry, and more particularly ecotourism (see Wearing 1995), is the link to professionalism. This has been the general pattern in other, related fields, including the recreation and leisure field, where debate has continued in the United States, according to Sessoms (1991), since the 1930s. (Currently, two organisations that drive certification efforts in the United States are the National Recreation and Park Association and the National Council for Therapeutic Recreation Certification).

Professionalism is viewed in essentially two ways. In one sense, the term implies only that one is paid for a service, as if, for example, a professional football player. It is, however, the stricter sense of 'profession' regarding conceptions surrounding occupations, such as lawyers and doctors, that is more difficult to define, and the focus of this section.

Foremost in the minds of professional groups and the lay public, the word 'professional' seems to be represented by two main themes, as suggested by Wilensky (1964 : 138): '(1) the job of the professional is technical—based on systematic knowledge or doctrine acquired only through long prescribed training; and (2) the professional man adheres to a set of *professional norms'*. In recreation, researchers and practitioners, historically, found it difficult to agree on a set of professional criteria to guide accepted practice. Professions therefore need to satisfy, and be consistent with, broad criteria in bonding the discipline together, as evident in the following work by Weschler (1962).

(1) The profession has a body of specialised knowledge.

(2) The profession sets its own standards.

(3) The profession requires extensive preparation.

(4) Specialised knowledge is communicable.

(5) Service is placed over personal gain.

(6) The profession has a strong professional organisation.

In recent years, university and college programmes in Canada have shown interest in addressing the issue of professionalism in the adventure tourism and ecotourism fields. The adventure Travel Guide Diploma programme of the University College of the Cariboo (UCC) in Kamloops, British Columbia, is one such programme that has been developed to prepare a more highly trained labour force in this area (Olesen and Schettini 1994). These authors rely on projections that suggest that the demand for highly trained personnel in the adventure tourism industry will grow at 3.6 per cent (compounded rate), which comparatively, far exceeds the anticipated 1.6 per cent yearly growth rates of the entire British Columbian labour force. This programme recognises the integral relationship between industry and government (and government-sponsored institutions) in certifying highly trained instructors, guides and operators. The UCC programme emphasises the following five main themes as being critical to the success of the programme: (1) technical skills (e.g. wilderness first aid training), (2) business skills, (3) hospitality and service skills, (4) environmental skills, and (5) intimate involvement in industry associations (e.g. student networks with potential employers).

The tourism field will have to come to grips with the notion of professionalism (whichever form this takes), given the tremendous interest in this area of late. One of the key elements to overcome in enabling the tourism worker to feel personally competent and confident in his or her work; as Wright (1987 : 17) points out, 'it is preferable to establish credibility through capability, competency, efficiency and a professional attitude. One earns respect, one does not establish respect through a glossy diploma on the wall'.

CONCLUSION

This chapter has illustrated that sound planning and management related to policy, regulation and accreditation, certification and professionalism are necessary considerations for the future viability of the ecotourism industry. While some governmental bodies have recognised early the importance of government leadership in the ecotourism industry, others have not been so quick to act. There must be both leadership and partnership between government and industry in the development of mechanisms to control the impact of ecotourism on the environment, and to ensure that operators are providing safe and enriching programmes to their clientele. Such mechanisms will most likely include policy, regulation, accreditation and professionalism in their various forms.

5

Ecology and Tourism Development

This chapter focuses on tourism development from three perspectives: international tourism development, including development theory, tourism in underdeveloped countries and the core-periphery concepts; community development; and site development. Each of the three offers frames of reference different from both the general tourism literature and ecotourism. While the international development literature provides a clear indication of where we have been in terms of tourism development, the community development or community-based ecotourism initiatives provide a contrasting view in support of where ecotourism should go in the future. The ecolodge phenomenon is included as an example of how site development can occur using sustainable development design principles and local decision-making.

International Issues

Development theory

> I sit on a man's back, choking him and making him carry me, and yet assure myself and others that I am very sorry for him and wish to ease his lot by any means possible, except getting off his back.
>
> Tolstoy

Development theory explores the economic and psychological link that exists between rich and poor countries. The relationship continues to be one that often contrasts meaning and value with respect to the use of natural resources and capital. Tourism is a sector of the world's economy that has tended to underscore and exacerbate the inequalities that exist between core metropolitan nations and peripheral, marginalised economies, and in doing so perpetuates the division between those who have access to resources and those who do not. To Vogeler and DeSouza (1980), this division has conjured up images of distorted human beings and grotesque folklorism, where the underdeveloped are like children unable to fend for themselves and with little capacity to make decisions.

Dependent countries were not considered economic entities until the late 1890s, when a new, 'lofty' responsibility regarding dependent peoples emerged (British Africa encouraged participation in the cash economy). This lofty purpose was coupled with a crude, hypocritical view of natives and administration, with the recognition that external power had a responsibility to develop the resources of dependent countries for the benefit of the whole world. Some saw the acquisition of overseas dominions as motivated by strategic reasons, while others sought only economic incentives (Brookfield 1975).

In measuring development, past research has used a variety of means to define it, including number of hospital beds, daily intake of calories, daily intake of animal protein, percentage of population in agriculture, food as a percentage of total imports, export economy, infant mortality, death rate and aid per capita. Many of these have been criticised owing to the fact that the socio-cultural, environment, and economic landscapes of each country are different. For example, food requirements are a cultural phenomenon, where countless generations have formed the habits of food intake seen today. Comparing the daily intake of calories between North Americans and Southeast Asians is pointless. Their physiological requirements are quite different (see Mountjoy 1971).

Resources have also been used to gauge the development status of nations, where an abundance of resources is thought to be an indicator of development. However, Mountjoy (1971) points out that even though Brazil has an abundance of resources and Denmark few, Denmark is considerably the more developed. Thus, development should be based not upon potential, but on existing levels of material welfare. Switzerland is a further case in point, where capital is a substitute for natural resource endowment. The progression of development, according to Brookfield (1975), occurred as a result to capitalist countries broadening on diversifying production into new sectors. This was to be achieved internationally through a widening of resource exploitation of less developed countries (LDCs). Brookfield maintains that the most aggressive industrial and trading nations (e.g. Britain) benefited most. They put pressure on other countries to open their trade. Adam Smith's *laissez-faire* philosophy was the true avenue of growth unfettered; it would work towards optimal production.

In recent years there has occurred a major paradigmatic revision in development thinking that is presenting a fundamental challenge to the conventional consensus on economic development. This new approach emphasises the basic needs of the poor, and advocates a sensitivity for development at the ground level. Real improvement cannot, therefore, occur in LDCs unless the strategies that are being formulated and implemented are environmentally sustainable (Barbier 1987). Brookfield (1975) emphasises support of this contention: the study of development joins directly with the study of all change in human use of the environment, and provides elements of empirical evidence for infusion with other theories in the task of generating a dynamic human-environment paradigm.

Mountjoy (1971) stipulates that the most important factors in gauging development are people; their number, age, enterprise, initiative, inventiveness, knowledge and willingness to sacrifice. It is not the responses themselves (which are passive), but the way in which they are to be utilised that is deterministic of development. The Western nations' concern for invention is not shared by all societies. Technologically inferior societies exploit single landscapes, within the framework of their social structures, while the Westerner is said to exploit all environments (*ibid.*). This is most clearly emphasised by the recent international debates on the implications of global warming for the future viability of the planet. LDCs make a strong case against the more industrialised developed nations for their role in the creation of the pollution (e.g. nitrogen oxide and sulphur dioxide emissions) that has contributed to global warming and ozone depletion.

Tourism in the Underdeveloped World

LDCs suffer from a history of colonial domination and what has been referred to as dependent development. A review of tourism literature reinforces the notion that there is a set evolutionary pattern of multinational interests in the tourism sector of the underdeveloped. Dependency, therefore, can be conceptualised as process of historical conditioning which alters the internal functioning of economic and social subsystems within a less developed country (Britton 1982). This dependency occurs not from processes within the LDC's economy, but rather from demand from overseas tourists and new foreign company investment in the LDC. For example, after a potential tourist destination has been identified (on the basis of unique biophysical or cultural conditions), the involvement of the multinationals increases. Foreign companies greatly influence the image of a destination country through development and promotion. Such efforts lead tourists to perceive the host country in terms of this image and the nature of hotel accommodation, attractions and other tourist services as publicised.

Domination of the tourism sector in an LDC is most outwardly represented by the foreign ownership of airlines and hotels. However, the grip on the destination region often goes much deeper. Because of the inability of agricultural and manufacturing producers in most underdeveloped economies to guarantee a good-quality supply of goods and services for international luxury-standard tourist facilities, there is a strong reliance on imported supplies for both the construction and the operation of tourist facilities. Also, as Winpenny (1982) writes, middle and senior management levels of tourism developments in underdeveloped countries are often occupied by expatriates. The following scenario of metropolitan dominance serves as an example:

> On arrival in a Caribbean island between plane and hotel, the tourists could well have passed through a terminal building presented by the people of Canada and have been driven along a road either built or improved 'thanks' to Canadian aid, on behalf of the expected Canadian tourists of course. At the hotel you will likely be greeted with rum punches the first of the few local products to be encompassed by the package. At your first meal, a menu, perhaps designed in Toronto, Chicago or Miami will provide you with a selection of food imported for the greater part from North America–good familiar, homogenized, taste-free food, dressed up with a touch of local colour. (Hills and Lundgren 1977 : 257)

The question therefore is as follows: who owns and controls the various components of a holiday package? It has been found (Economic and Social Commission for Asia and the Pacific 1978: 40) that where tour packages consist to a foreign air carrier, but include local hotel and other groups services, destination countries receive on average only 40-45 per cent of the inclusive tour retail prices paid by the tourists in their home country. If both the airline and hotels are owned by foreign companies, a mere 22–25 per cent of the retail tour price stays in the destination country.

While Rajotte (1980) feels that tourism is less environmentally destructive than other forms of development that exist in tropical islands, there are still many significant effects that may be attributed to tourism. Many of these impacts are universal, but their intensity and severity are more noticeable in island environments (much of the past research on dependency and development has been linked to island environments). Important is the notion that often with size comes ecological diversity. Nation states of the Caribbean, because of their small size, have tenuous floral and faunal vitality. Tourism can stress these systems through yearly visitation levels that exceed the local population of an island; for example, Hayward *et al.* (1981) write that in 1979, more than 600,000 tourists visited Bermuda, some ten times the population of the island.

A key area of research for the future is the need to document whether or not developing countries such as Brazil, Costa Rica, Dominica, the countries of Eastern Africa, and Ecuador undergo the same social, ecological, and economic dysfunctions from ecotourism as outlined above from the perspective of mass tourism. For example, Kusler (1991) writes that ecotourism in the LDCs is marked by limited dollars, government-directed financing, foreign visitation, foreign ownership of hotels and other facilities, and non-existent land use planning. In this sense, ecotourism as an intervention may or may not improve the socio-economic conditions of a country from the example of mass tourism outlined above. It is important to realise, as outlined by Kusler, that the LDCs and their developed-country counterparts are separated by a number of key structural differences. These include finances, the political climate of a country, accessibility to opportunities, discretionary income, and resources for the acquisition and planning of land.

Core-periphery Concept

One of the main theoretical approaches used to explain development is the concept of core and periphery, which Freidmann and Alonso (1974) describe as characterised by a dynamic, growing central region, and a slower-growing or stagnating periphery. The core is marked by high-growth potential whereas peripheral areas are often marked by declining rural economies with low agricultural production (loss of primary resource). Shields (1991 : 3) refers to peripheralized regions as marginal places, regions that 'are not necessarily on geographical peripheries but, first and foremost, they have been placed on the periphery of cultural systems of space in which places are ranked relative to each other'. Important in his discussion is the fact that margins, from social, political, economic and perceptual perspectives, are systems of centres and peripheries and are, therefore, locationally oriented. These spatial systems are established in a series of binary relationships (economic, society, and so on) of centre and periphery, so that margins signify everything that the centre denies or represses (Shields 1991). Our socio-economic paradigm is constantly exercising this binary relationship, and it reaches to the furthest outposts of physical space and humanity.

In a touristic sense, a classic example of the core-periphery idea can be found in Christaller's (1963) analysis of tourism location in Europe (see Chapter 2 and the discussion on the evolving nature of tourists within destinations). Christaller wrote that tourism avoids central places and is drawn to the periphery, reaching the natural resource base not found in cities. This idea has been further developed by a number of authors (Butler 1980; Pearce 1989). In particular, Battisti (1982) reflected on the principles established by Christaller on tourist space organisation, noting that tourism is part of the continual process carried out by humankind in order to specialise and to diversify the exploitation of the soil. Battisti made reference to the distinction between peripheral regions and peripheral places. The first represents a wide range of possibilities in choosing a recreational place. The second indicates real destinations of tourist flows, where the 'fruition of space for recreational purposes is accomplished' (*ibid.*: 60).

The core-periphery concept has also been applied more recently to the analysis of adventure travel regions from a spatial context. Zurick (1992) suggested that the movement of adventure travellers in Nepal takes place through a complicated hierarchy of gateways. Tourists from the core move through an international gateway (semi-periphery), to a national gateway (periphery), and further to a regional gateway (periphery frontier), said to be the adventure region. In this latter region there is often a clash between traditional interests and national development goals. As frontier regions succumb to further intrusions, the uniqueness of these areas diminishes, as does the potential for travel to untouched areas in the future as these areas become fewer in number.

One of the key defining elements of travellers to outward peripheries is the need to experience something different in a remote setting. Along with this, perhaps, is the need to escape the mainstream of tourism, which can only be achieved by taking the road less travelled. Although there are few data at hand to support this idea the traveller's mind-set may alter upon reaching successive outward peripheries of a destination. Fennell (1996) thought that the following factors contributed to this feeling:

- *Familiarity with the destination*—A lack of knowledge or familiarity with a region's environment/culture may add to the uniqueness of such an area and therefore represent a perceived periphery.
- *Unscheduled change*—Movement that occurs spontaneously or that is not pre-planned (e.g. from a core region to a peripheral region).
- *Psychological and/or physiological change*—Personal adaptations that have to be made in order to feel comfortable or maximise feelings of satisfaction/pleasure, including culture, language, personal hygiene, food and shelter.
- *Distance from amenities*—This factor reinforces the notion that a particular peripheral region does not, cannot, or will not offer goods and services that can be found at regions closer to the core.
- *Adaptation*—As tourists move out to a new periphery, the accompanying shortage of goods and services such as shops

and facilities–found at regions closer to the core–becomes more accepted. The state of the infrastructure, therefore, plays less of a role in satisfying the tourist. Poor weather may also not pose a problem because a more 'frontier-like' attitude is adopted.

- *Population density*—Regions with a lower tourist and local population density may provide an indication that the periphery has been, or is being, reached.
- *Authenticity*—As population density decreases, the authenticity and/or incidence of natural and cultural attractions may increase in relation to the characteristics of the region. The character of the region is important, as Costa Rica may have a higher species diversity in urban areas than Shetland has at the periphery.
- *Symbolism*—The periphery may be represented by experiential, environmental, or cultural phenomena (symbols). Such phenomena may include lochs, mountains, wind, solitude, barrenness, a rainforest, or lack of banking machines. Consequently, the more these symbols are experienced, the greater might be the feeling of reaching the perimeter. Fear may also act as a symbol, as may the realisation that there is a lack of knowledge of a region and its characteristics. Fear or anxiety of the unknown is an important feature of adventure tourism (characteristics that Csikszentmihalyi (1990) has reported on regarding risk-taking in rock climbers).
- *Scale of attraction*—It is the region itself that may take on characteristics of 'attraction' in the outer periphery. For example, while cities have many attractions and goods and services to offer tourists and local alike, small, peripheral islands may have comparatively few or no structural attractions, and because of this the nature of the island's limited infrastructure, small size, and distance from the mainland may be the attraction itself.
- *Distance from home*—This factor occurs in combination with other factors. For example, travel to Sydney, Australia, from rural Canada represents a large distance, but may not necessarily represent a mental change from core to periphery.

Thus, the relationship between core and periphery has not only a psychological component but, as discussed earlier, a spatial one. This spatial component occurs at a variety of scales. Examples include small islands of the South controlled by the North, and huge territories of the North controlled politically, economically, and socially by decision-makers of the core. The Northwest Territories of Canada has been identified by Keller (1987) as an example of a peripheral region caught in transition regarding the development of its tourism industry. To Keller, differing authorities in control of development in this region become important actors in both decision-making and implementation of a viable tourist industry. These hierarchies of control occur at local, regional, national and international levels. As the sphere of tourism development becomes international, Keller suggests, the more the periphery has become 'a playground for exogenous investors, and the peripheral government an observer of its own fate' (*ibid.*: 25). It is stated by keller that to avoid a transgression of the above scenario, the periphery (Northwest Territories) must act to control the decision-making in the development of a tourist industry, and limit the development to a scale of growth in tune with the resources, capital, manpower, and culture within the periphery.

The implications of the core-periphery concept to ecotourism are that, often, remote travel regions are dependent on national and international markets, inbound and outbound tour operators, as well as externally based transport modes and schedules. With the inability and lack of resources fully to plan and implement Ecotourism on their own, the cycle of tourism dependency continues for peripheral regions. This lack of an ability to link directly with the market in the developed world is one of the main reasons why the benefits of ecotourism do not percolate down to the community level; and it is precisely why those who are able to coordinate ecotourism activities–whether they be expatriates or local–between the LDCs and the developed world stand greatly to gain economically. In such a case the power to make ecotourism happen in a developing country lies in the hands of a few, and perpetuates the phenomenon of a typical LDC economic situation, with much of the money and resources lying in the hands of a few, and the majority of the population, in the absence of a prominent middle class, living in impoverished conditions.

While the preceding discussion has emphasised the significance and impact of externally based control in the development of tourism and ecotourism enterprises at a macro level, the discussion of community development to follow offers an alternative to many of the tourism development concerns outlined above. Community development, then, may be considered as a viable means by which to offset the conventional tourism development models of the past and redistribute control and decision-making among the individuals within the community, not to those from outside.

Community Development

Community development, as described by Smith (1990a), originated in the self-help programmes that were developed during the depression years in Canada, the United States and the United Kingdom. A defining characteristic of community development is that it is based on local initiatives, in that it advocates a site-specific approach to finding solutions to community problems using community members and community resources. Bujold (1995 : 5) defines it as 'the process by which the efforts of the people themselves are united with those of governmental authorities to improve economic, social, and cultural conditions of communities'. Typical community development encompasses all aspects of the community and focuses on the best quality of life possible for its members (Davidson 1995), and may involve creating new business and employment, increasing cultural awareness, or providing a range of opportunities for all members of the community. However, Joppe (1996) alludes to the fact that it is important to understand that there exists a fundamental division between conventional community development and community economic development (CED) models. While conventional economic development focuses on the attraction of new businesses to the community (seen as an outward-directed approach to development), conversely a CED focus is on being small, green, and social, and is more inward in its orientation by striving to 'help consumers become producers, users become providers, and employees become owners of enterprise' (Joppe 1996: 476), through the principles of economic self-reliance, ecological sustainability, community control, meeting individual needs and building a community culture.

Tourism is increasingly seen as a key community development tool in the 1990s, with the recognition of its economic contribution in bolstering stangnating economies and diversifying existing sectors, and its ability to unify community members. Such is the case in the Shetland Islands, Scotland, where tourism is being relied upon to sustain an economy that was once dominated by North Sea oil development (Butler and Fennell 1994), or the Finnish island of Aland, where all tourism initiatives are owned or controlled by local people (Joppe 1996). With this realisation, researchers have begun to explore community development as it relates to tourism and ecotourism from many different perspectives. As an example, Christensen (1995) examines the role that tourism can play in securing quality of life within the community. At the foundation of any tourism development strategy is the realisation that :

> If tourism development is to be viable as a long-term economic strategy, these concerns [social and ecological] must be addressed, and the resource base must be protected in the process. The host community is the economic, social, cultural, and infrastructural resource base for most tourism activity, and resident quality of life is a measure of the condition of the resource. (Christensen 1995 : 63)

Christensen proposes a community quality of life framework that addresses both objective and subjective indicators, at the individual and community scale. A tourism development project is said to affect change in the quality of life of members of the community, which in turn cause impacts at different social scales. Such impacts need to be evaluated both by individuals and by the community, depending on the scale of reference to the individual. There is a deliberate hierarchy established with respect to agents of change, suggesting that appropriate solutions need to be implemented at the individual social scale first, followed by neighbourhood groups, coalitions, responsible industry, policy and governmental regulation.

The tactical approaches used by regions (local or national governing bodies) will make or break how ecotourism is perceived by local people, according to MacKinnon (1995). She sites a number of examples of communities in Mexico which have adopted or been identified to develop ecotourism in the country. One such community is Tres Garantias in the Yucatán peninsula. This region was initially set out as a hunting reserve by an international development team, but the area's residents found that non-consumptive recreation was more attractive to tourists than consumptive forms. The project, however, was conceived using a top-end approach, and even though there have been isolated benefits derived from ecotourism, MacKinnon suggests that social integration within the community is not complete, and will not be complete until benefits are more widespread and the perception of ownership is given to the community. MacKinnon further uses the example of Los Tuxtlas, Veracruz, to illustrate that ecotourism has been successfully integrated into a community through more of a grassroots approach (initiated through the efforts of a local woman who set out to build empowerment slowly and deliberately). In this later case, the community has been more quickly able to realise benefits which have been spreading on a more regional scale. According to MacKinnon, the traditional mass tourism development model perpetuates the widening gap between rich and poor in countries like Mexico. Conversely, community-based tourism 'lends itself to being environmentally sustainable. Locals are the first to recognize the benefits of conserving their natural-resource base–much more so than large developers who don't live in the area' (MacKinnon 1995: 47).

While the interests of the community from a social standpoint are certainly paramount in the development of small-scale ecotourism, Williams (1992) feels that all factions within the community need to cooperate effectively in ensuring that a high-quality product is delivered without diminishing the ecology of the resource base. He advocates the development of an institutional structures strategy with the capacity to respond to tourism development before such development runs out of control. This strategy includes the following—

(1) development of a grassroots planning process, driven by local interests and including aboriginal involvement;

(2) understanding and appreciation of ecotourism market requirements;

(3) an inventory of the region's resources to determine areas that are suitable for ecotourism and ones that are not;

(4) the establishment of goals and objectives in line with concerns related to the cultural and natural impacts of ecotourism, with the creation of a vision statement to act as a control mechanism for the future; and

(5) the establishment of a formal Tourism Management Board, to work with both the operators and the public, with the responsibility of monitoring change, communication, local benefits, etc.

Despite the fact that there will be direct and indirect beneficiaries and participants in the ecotourism industry, it is important to recognise that the entire community should be involved to some level. Participation therefore plays a key role in the initiative, as it empowers people to play a role in the decision-making process, where in many cases it is only those who are politically connected or affluent who are involved in the control and management of the enterprise (Sproule 1996). Such involvement can take the form of community representatives who speak for various elements of the population. This 'management committee' is very much like the proposed Tourism Management Board outlined by Williams (1992). The community ecotourism initiative needs to be founded on the notion of trust and transparency. Actions and decisions need to be communicated to the community through bulletin boards or other means. Money and finances are identified by Sproule as critical elements in dividing a community. To be open about expenditures and to share information in an attempt to dispel feelings of mismanagement or corruption is to be transparent in one's approach to management. Specifically, Sproule's community-based ecotourism (CBE) refers to

> ecotourism enterprises that are owned and managed by the community. Furthermore, community-based ecotourism implies that a community is taking care of their natural resources in order to gain income through operating a tourism enterprise and using that income to better their lives. It involves conservation, business enterprise and community development. (Sproule 1996 : 3)

A final example of how management may be used to control the development of ecotourism initiatives within a community is outlined by Drake (1991). She defines local participation as 'the ability of local communities to influence the outcome of development projects such as ecotourism that have an impact on them' (*ibid.* : 132). Important in this process is the demonstrated benefit to the community both through community members' participation and through their realisation that some aspect of their community has been treated or protected (e.g. natural resources). The following is proposed as a model of local participation in the development of ecotourism projects (*ibid.*: 149-155):

- *Phase 1–Determine the role of local participation in project*—This includes an assessment of how local people can help achieve set goals through efficiency, increasing project effectiveness, building beneficiary capacity and sharing project costs.
- *Phase 2–Choose research team*—The team should include a broad multidisciplinary approach and include people in the social sciences and those within the media.
- *Phase 3–Conduct preliminary studies*—Political, economic and social conditions of the community should be studied in the context of the environment, from existing documents, and by other survey-related work. Identification and assessment of the following is important: needs, key local leaders, media, the community's commitment to the project, intersectoral involvement, traditional uses of the land, the type of people interested in the project and why, the role of women, who will manage and finance the project, land ownership and cultural values.
- *Phase 4–Determine the level of local involvement*—Local involvement occurs along a continuum from low-intensity to high-intensity involvement. This must be determined in addition to when the involvement is to occur. In cases where government is not supportive of local government, intermediaries (e.g. NGOs) can be used to facilitate local participation.

- *Phase 5–Determine an appropriate participation mechanism*—This is affected by the level of intensity of the participation, the nature of existing institutions (e.g. government, NGOs, citizens' groups), and the characteristics of the local people (how vociferous they may or may not be). This phase may include information sharing and consultation, which usually takes the form of a citizen advisory committee with representatives from many groups within the community. The committee is charged with the task of commenting on goals and objectives or other project-related aspects.
- *Phase 6–Initiating dialogue and educational efforts*—The use of the press is important in this phase as a means by which to build consensus through public awareness. Key community representatives can be used in this process. The ecotourism team should explain the goals and objectives of the project, how the project will affect the community, the values of the area, any history of threats, and the benefits of the project. Various audiovisual techniques should be used to emphasise these points. Workshops or public meetings could be organised to identify strengths and weaknesses of the project.
- *Phase 7–Collective decision-making*—This is a critical stage that synthesises all research and information from the local population. The ecotourism project team present the findings of their research to the community, together with an action plan. Community members are asked to react to the plan, with the possible end result being a forum through which the team and local people negotiate to reach a final consensus based on the impacts of the project.
- *Phase 8–Development of an action plan and implementation scheme*—In this phase, the team and community develop an action plan for implementing solutions to identified problems. For example, if members of the community express the need to increase the community's standard of living, the team may respond by purchasing agricultural produce from local people at market rates or on a contractual basis. They may also develop a variety of positions to be occupied by local people including gift shops, research positions, park management positions, and private

outfitting companies for the local people. This local action plan must then be integrated into the broader master plan of the project.

- *Phase 9–Monitoring and evaluation*—Monitoring and evaluation, although often neglected, should occur-frequently and over the long term. The key to evaluation is to discover whether goals and objectives set out early in the project's life cycle have been accomplished or not.

Community development initiatives have a better chance of being accepted by local people if developers being to acknowledge the fact that different groups within the community want different things, depending on their role in, affinity within, and utilisation of the community. This perspective is discussed by Jurowski (1996), who feels that because the impacts of tourism are not the same for all residents, residents' individual values need to be recognised by tourism developers in order for their projects to be successful.

The first unique group identified by Jurowski is the 'attached resident'. Such a person is likely to be a long-term resident or an older individual who loves living in the community because of its social and physical benefits. To these people, control over the form and function of their community is important. In general, tourism developers can gain support for their projects from this group by involving citizens in the planning process, establishing a focal point and common theme, developing projects that emphasise heritage themes, and showing that the project has social and ecological benefits for the community.

The second type established by Jurowski, the 'resource user', typically includes people like anglers and other recreationists who, although ambivalent about the economic impacts of tourism, can be won over by developers. The developers can gain their support by providing skill opportunities for youth, involving this group in events related to their interests (e.g. bike races), protecting 'their' sites for participation, and allocating tourism funds for the development of facilities and services they desire.

The final group outlined by Jurowski is the 'environmentalist'. Although this group is the most likely to focus on the negative aspects of the development, it is in the best interests of development teams to do the following: (1) provide information on how the project will protect the environment; (2) incorporate ecological education programmes; (3) encourage the participation of environmentalists in development; and (4) prompt citizens to develop their own educational programmes for tourists. Projects that reflect the interests and concerns of the community, therefore, are said generally to stimulate volunteer activity and minimise conflict.

This research is attractive because it acknowledges that people residing in the local community are indeed different from one another. This is in contrast to much tourism research which considers the local community as one homegeneous group (see also the work of Weaver and Wishard-Lambert 1996).

A key principle underlying the process of community development is the element of leadership. Mabey (1994) suggests that unlike the older model of leadership, seen as an individual influencing a group towards an end, newer leadership paradigms involve collaboration and partnerships between community individuals, groups and organisations. This means devolving power to the followers, according to Mabey, and being fluid in the connection of people and resources. Belasco and Stayer (1993: 18) linked this new style of leadership to what happens in a flight of geese:

> I could see the geese flying in their 'V' formation, the leadership changing frequently, with different geese taking the lead. I saw every goose being responsible for getting itself wherever the gaggle was going, changing roles whenever necessary, alternating as a leader, a follower or a scout . . . .I could see each goose being a leader.

This example illustrates the importance of a common purpose in removing obstacles and establishing responsibility within the community ecotourism initiative. In essence the process of empowerment-holding the will, resources, and opportunity to make decisions within the community–allows people, either internal or external to the community, to step in and provide assistance in a respectful manner, while allowing local people to shape and control the pace of tourism development within their communities. Where this is especially relevant is in marginal places where there exists a tremendous void between those who can and those who cannot access information and resources. As such, education must play a key role in this empowerment process of revitalisation through ecotourism (e.g. providing the needed means to enable people to be informed to certain choices). An excellent example of eduction's role in empowerment lies in the Community Baboon Sanctuary project of Belize. Through education and partnerships, local farmers have stopped their conventional practice of clearing and denuding the land for agriculture purposes in favour of a land management strategy that is more environmentally sound. In so doing they have been able to attract international tourists fascinated by the ecological and cultural diversity of this part of the world (Lipske 1992). Education, therefore, helps to rekindle people's love and appreciation of the land, which is indeed important for both community-building and nation-building. A similar case study involves the Havasupai reservation adjacent to the Grand Canyon National Park in northern Arizona, where education and tourism have played a significant role in diversifying the local economy (White 1993).

Partnerships

A partnership, as defined by Uhlik (1995 : 14) is 'an on-going arrangement between two or more parties, based upon satisfying specifically identified, mutual needs. Such partnerships are characterized by durability over time, inclusiveness, cooperation and flexibility.' More specifically, Uhlik (1995) developed a six-stage model of partnership development that concentrates on the conditions that will lead to a successful partnership agreement. These include (1) education of self and others; (2) needs assessment and resource inventory; (3) identifying prospective partners and investigating their needs and inventories; (4) comparing and contrasting needs and resources; (5) developing a partnership proposal; and (6) proposing a partnership.

Clements *et al.* (1993) suggest that because tourism is starting to be recognized as a community development tool, development must be sensitive to the requirements of many stakeholder groups, including tourism providers (e.g. hotels), public providers (e.g. recreation and park providers), and residents. Their view is that partnerships must be struck to ensure that a high-quality product is delivered, and is based on the notion that tourism experiences rely on all aspects of the community. The overall effectiveness of the delivery system is only as strong as its weakest link, and communities intent on the development of a tourism industry will increasingly nearly on the positive benefits of partnerships in being accountable to the local and non-local public.

The partnerships developed for ecotourism, according to Sproule (1996), must also fit into systems that have been developed at regional and national levels. There are potentially many partnerships that can be struck to facilitate an atmosphere of cooperation and trust. Potential partners include: (1) organisations within the established tourism industry, particularly tour operators; (2) the government tourism bureau and natural resource agencies, especially the park service; (3) non-governmental organisations (NGOs), especially those involved with environmental issues, small business management, and traditional community development; (4) universities and other research organisations; (5) other communities, including those with a history of tourism and also those that are just beginning; and (6) other international organisations, public and private funding institutions, national cultural committees, and many others; the tourism industry literature is replete with examples of stakeholder groups that have conventionally been at odds. In Canada, the United States, Australia, and many other countries around the world, there exists a significant degree of incompatibility between parks and aboriginal peoples. McNeely (1993) feels that despite what has occurred in the past, partnerships must be forged between these two groups in order that both may prosper in the late twentieth century and beyond. He feels that the following ten principles must be followed in order to help the cooperative efforts of these stakeholder groups (*ibid.*: 253):

(1) Build on the foundations of local culture.

(2) Give responsibility to local people.

(3) Consider returning ownership of at least some protected areas to indigenous people.

(4) Hire local people.

(5) Link government development programmes with protected areas.

(6) Give priority to small-scale local development.
(7) Involve local people in preparing management plans.
(8) Have the courage to enforce restrictions.
(9) Build conservation into the evolving new national cultures.
(10) Support diversity as a value.

Rather than emphasise what has not worked in the past, the partnership ideal must embrace the present and future needs of the groups involved in any transaction. For those in the realm of parks it may be biodiversity and the establishment of more protected area. From the perspective of aboriginal people, decision-making and culture may be issues that top the list.

Aboriginal Interests

As outlined above, the relationship between parks and aboriginal people has often been one based on conflict, and stems from the physical displacement and socio-economic fragmentation of aboriginal people. In Canada, the relationship has been one of mistrust, where peripheral lands (occupied by aboriginals) have been run outside the control and sphere of influence of local native authority. This in itself is a perpetuation of the rift that has existed between Ottawa in the south and those living in the 'north'. Part of the problem exists because the concept of 'park' never existed in aboriginal languages, at least in North America, and the fundamentals of our Western view of park management (i.e. balancing recreational use with preservation) are completely alien to aboriginal culture, as outlined by Notzke:

> The distinction between work and leisure is largely an artifact of industrial society. The fragmentation and compartmentalisation of life and environment which is part and parcel of western culture, is totally alien to aboriginal cosmologies, which view the world in an essentially holistic and unified manner. (Notzke 1994:1)

This view is supported by Sadler (1989), who suggests that aboriginals think of space primarily from a holistic perspective, which is contrary to the dichotomous Western perspective associated with conservation. Park management therefore proceeded to exclude Aboriginals entirely from the park planning process. This has led to an indifferent, even hostile, attitude towards the existence of parks close to or adjacent to aboriginal lands. The Clearwater River Provincial Park in northwestern Saskatchewan is an example of this indifference. Even though there is an abundant population of indigenous people in the vicinity of the park, there is little use of park resources (e.g. fish, game) by such people, in large part because of the park's political status (B. Wilson, personal communication, December 4, 1996). In order for parks to become accepted by the aboriginal population, therefore, some feel that a revision must be made to the preservation mandate that currently exists in some types of parks, changing it to one that is conservation oriented, which will be more consistent with the social, economic, and ecological requirements of the First Nations people in Canada.

CASE STUDY 5.1

The Struggle for Kakadu

According to Fox (1996), territories rich in resources provide more options for their use. This is the case with Kakadu National Park in the Northern Territory of Australia, which is a World Heritage Site and a place of immense ecological and cultural significance, Kakadu is owned by the Aborigines of the region, who lease it to the National Park Service. Legally mismanagement of the resource may lead to the tenure being terminated. Ecotourism is thriving in the park, so much so that according to the Aborigines, there is no longer a distinction being made between the effects of mining and tourism; both are contributing to the degradation of the park. Some Aboriginal people, according to Fox, recognise that while mining will ultimately end, tourism will continue to grow and grow, and has manifested itself in the form of planned multi-million dollar tourism projects for the park. The issue of most concern to Aborigines is that their fundamental values are not consistent with current development philosophies in the park. According to Elliot (1991), the example of mining and tourism in Kakadu is a perfect example of the competing and overlapping environmental values that various stakeholders have. For example, would it matter if our actions caused a species to become extinct? Would it matter if our actions caused the death of individual animals? Would is matter if we caused widespread erosion in the park? Is the extinction of a species an acceptable price to pay for increased employment opportunities? One would imagine that miners, the tourism industry, Aborigines, the park service, and other interests would all differ along these fundamental lines.

The element of control is critical in analysing any relationship between the ecotourism industry and indigenous people. For tourism development to be successful, aboriginal people must be allowed to take control of it despite the social and political forces that often work against them. This has been a problem in the restructuring of South Africa, where there remains a legacy of poor education and lack of training for black people (Swart and Saayman 1997). The result is that the whole touristic experience is one that is inherently foreign to the poor in South African society. Given that part of the government's tourism vision relates to addressing the need to improve the quality of life of every South African, Swart and Saayman recognise the need for significant changes in legislation to benefit all people.

Keller (1987), as discussed earlier, recognised that the Northwest Territories (NWT) has struggled with the development of its tourism industry, largely owing to the real lack of control of the industry at the local and regional levels. Keller's conclusions imply that the people of this peripheral region must have decision-making control and act to limit development to a scale of growth in tune with the social, ecological and economic climate of the region. However, at least in some places in the NWT, Inuit, Indians and Metis people have started to realise that their varying social, ecological and economic needs can best be met through cooperative action with other agencies. The vehicle that is enabling them to do this is national parks, territorial parks, heritage rivers, and the tourism opportunities that emerge from such areas. For example, Seale (1992) suggests that two rivers, the Thelon and the Kazan, where easily designated as within the Canadian Heritage Rivers system owing to the fact that the project planner lived within the community with his family for 18 months, in an attempt to educate and work closely with local organisations such as the Hunters and Trappers Association and the Elders' Society. Seale believes that continued success will be contingent upon recognising the importance of conservation, tourism, and the needs of aboriginal people in Canada's north. In particular the following factors need to be considered—

Community Involvement

- Involvement of First Nations people in all aspects of tourism and conservation planning.

Community Benefits

- Continued and/or exclusive access to biophysical resources of the protected area for subsistence purposes.

- Provision of technical and professional training opportunities relating to positions in tourism and in conservation agencies.
- Priority status in hiring programmes undertaken by tourism interests and conservation agencies.
- Priority status in the licensing of businesses to be operated in the park or protected area.
- Compilation of traditional knowledge and heritage values of the aboriginal societies by the conservation jurisdiction, for use both by the communities themselves in strengthening their societal traditions, and by the conservation agency in managing the protected area and in giving to its visitors a heightened appreciation of the traditional society.

Scale

- Ecotourism and adventure tourism can be accommodated much more readily than mass tourism, where control of such tourists (numbers and use patterns) will be in the communities' best interests socially and ecologically.

Land Ownership

- Tourism and protected areas will be accepted much more readily by aboriginal societies if the legal status of the land in question is first settled to their satisfaction.

Sensitivity to Needs of Area Residents and Visitors

- Ecotourists must be informed as to what is and what is not acceptable behaviour in the north, in recognising that the quality of their experience depends in part on their compliance to accepted norms.
- Traditional societies and conservation organisations need to come together to establish patterns in which visitors and locals can meet in circumstances of mutual respect.

Increasingly, however, examples in the literature are emerging that demonstrate the positive signs of local indigenous control in the ecotourism industry. For example, Hitchcock (1993) illustrates that the semi-nomadic pastoralist people of Purros in Namibia have been able to develop of successful ecotourism industry. Ecotourists are asked to pay the equivalent of about US $12 to enter their tribal area, with all the money generated from tourism being divided equally among members of the community. Other aspects of the ecotourism initiative include (1) the fact that tourists must abide by structured guidelines (developed by the local people); (2) tour guiding and handicraft prices are set, so as to avoid undercutting; and (3) programmes to educate tourists on resource use in the area have been set up. Such community

Table 5.1
Code for the Indigenous-sensitive Ecotourist

- Who operates the programme. Is it indigenous-run? If so, is it operated communally or do only a few individuals or families profit?
- If not indigenous-run, do local communities receive an equitable share of the profits or any other direct benefits, such as training? Or do only a few individuals/families benefit?
- Learn as much as you can about the local culture and customs. Visit local indigenous federation offices for information and materials with an indigenous perspective.
- Do not take photographs without asking permission.
- If you want to give a gift, make it a useful gift to the community rather than to an individual (e.g. gift to a school). Most indigenous communities function communally.
- Refrain from tipping individuals. If you are with a group, everyone can contribute to a gift to the community.
- Be aware of the boundaries of individual homes and gardens. Never enter or photograph without permission.
- Bring your own water purification tablets. Don't rely on boiling water exclusively as it depletes fuelwood and contributes to forest destruction.
- Pack out what you take in, and use biodegradable soaps.
- Be sensitive to those around you.
- Don't make promises you cannot or will not keep–for example, sending back photos to local people.
- Do not collect plants or plant products without permission.
- Wear appropriate and discreet clothing (e.g. many cultures are offended by women in shorts even though they may go topless).
- Respect local residents' privacy and customs. Treat people with the respect you would expect from visitors to your own home.

Sources : Colvin 1994.

action, according to Hitchcock, is definitely on the rise in the developing world. Following point 1 above, Colvin (1994) proposes a code of ethics for the indigenous-sensitive ecotourist as set out in Table 5.1.

The issue of control in the development of ecotourism was at the centre of an incident between the Kuna Indians of Panama and the Panama national government. Chapin (1990) writes that in the 1970s the government of Panama had the specific aim of working with multinational corporations in the development of a tourism product in the region of the Kuna (around Carti on the Caribbean side of the country): 'In return for their services as tourist attractions, the Kuna were to be given employment as service staff' (Chapin 1990 : 43). According to Chapin, the Kuna were unwilling to comply with the feasibility team and collectively forced the tourism industry influence out of the region. While plans for the development of casinos had to be discarded, one operator had his boat confiscated, and another individual had to endure being shot, set on fire, a hanging attempts, and a pummelling at the hands of many Kuna youth. Conversely, the small hotels of the region that currently exist in the area are all run by Kuna and cater to a small and manageable number of tourists on the basis of Kuna ownership and Kuna law. Communities are therefore cognisant of the importance of sustainable development and are striving to achieve it, but under the following conditions: (1) they must have control of the industry; (2) projects must be small in size and therefore manageable; and (3) there must be equity and dialogue among the various stakeholders.

The importance of training and education appears to be a common thread that links the literature on ecotourism and indigenous development. Wearing (1994) emphasises that at any level of hierarchy, 'ordinary' people are perfectly able to solve their own problems if given the chance. Through an analysis of ecotourism and local indigenous communities, Wearing believes that experiential education and training are crucial in allowing such communities to develop ecotourism so that it is not just another commodified product where benefits are exported and natural resources are abused (Fig. 5.1). 'Concrete experiences' are important in acting as cornerstones to teaching and learning in many idigenous communities. Aboriginal people can contrast this with the 'formation of abstract concepts and generalisations' attitude, which is more akin to the Western approach, and provides the means by which to bring a more conceptual foundation to the learning process. 'Observations and reflections' and 'testing implications of concepts in new situations,' represent the integration of Western and local traditions that may be desired of an ecotourism experience, with the former representing a traditional method of learning in aboriginal cultures and the latter representing more of a Western scientific approach to problem-solving.

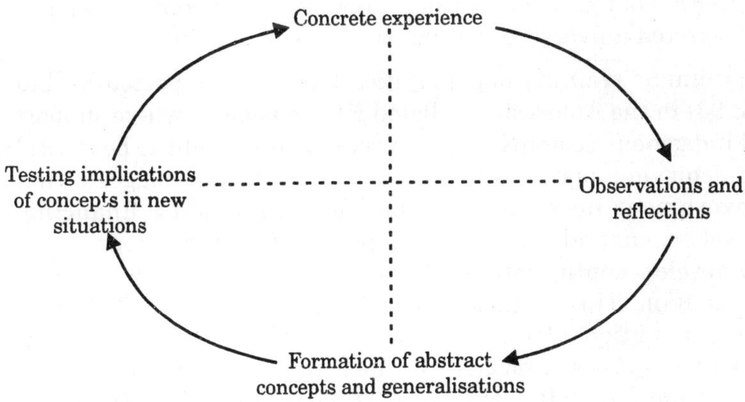

Fig. 5.1 : Model of ecotourism educational training.

A significant body of research has surfaced in Australia on parks and aboriginal involvement, where despite many years of agreements and talks, there still exists uncertainty regarding the role that Aboriginals must play within protected areas. In Kakadu, Cobourg and Uluru national parks, reported to be the model of Aboriginal-national parks relations in Australia, co-management strategies have not been successful in integrating and protecting indigenous values and rights (Cordell 1993), despite the fact that land in these areas has been given back to Aboriginals as freehold title. Davey (1993) reports that the models break done by failing to involve the aboriginal landowners in policy and planning, by not having majority Aboriginal representation on park boards, and by the lack of training and skills to enable Aboriginal people better to understand their role within the park setting. Notwithstanding these failures, Australians have endeavoured to overcome some of these problems through research initiatives designed to develop Aboriginal skills and training. Baker *et al.*, (1992) suggest that Aboriginal people can contribute equally to park management by applying Aboriginal ecological knowledge–which is based on generations of accumulated knowledge–with conventional biological surveys to overcome the time and finance constraints normally associated with research. In addressing the need to enhance Aboriginal skill levels (outlined above). De Lacy (1992) discusses the development of a number of Aboriginal employment programmes in Australia in the 1980s, including the initiation of many courses and skills that are currently available at selected universities within the Australian system.

Similar training opportunities have been reported by Liu (1994) in the American Affiliated Pacific Islands, where support of indigenous ecotourism entrepreneurs is thought to be critical in achieving sustainable economic growth. Liu suggests that government needs to take the lead in providing financing, development and operational support, and training programmes to develop appropriate marketing and business skills for this population. This is supported by King and Stewart (1996), who feel that national level controls are needed, in concert with local involvement, as a means by which to coordinate ecotourism development with the aim of reducing the effects of commodification of local indigenous cultures.

Site Development

The tourism industry has long been recognised as a formidable agent of social and ecological change, some say in a positive context through increased education, renewed pride in culture, the conservation of heritage, and of course economics (Lickorish 1991), while others say in a negative sense, at the expense of people and the resource base. For example, hotel developments in Spain and Turkey have been identified as being excessive in their impacts on beach environments. In other cases, improper development and the lack of sewerage systems hamper the tourism industry to such an extent in places in Mexico and Brazil that tourists are told not to swim in the ocean owing to the pollution. In such cases tourism development is strongly affected by what does not exist (i.e. no sewerage systems) or because such systems are unable to keep pace with the ongoing increase in tourism visitation and associated development.

The style and extent of tourism development in the 1990s has been tempered by the trend towards the increase in the recent past, in mega-development projects designed to cater to a growing market of travellers looking for self-contrained, hassle-free vacations. Fennell (1989) writes that this mega-resort boom began in the mid-1980s, and includes sites such as the 31,000 acre resort community of Waikoloa in Hawaii and the 1,200 acre Sanctuary Cove mixed-use resort between Brisbane and the Gold Coast. Yet while most of the development has been centred in what have been politically stable democracies, management consultants have been looking to the untapped markets of the Far East (Fennell 1989; see also Ayala 1996).

In the midst of this mega-development push there has emerged the move towards more responsible travel and development, in response to the green movement (pressure from various groups including academics, ENGOs, and the general public), and in keeping one step ahead of the competition. The response to the changing emphasis has meant that even some of the major hotel chains have endeavoured to experiment with ecologically sound rooms through recycling, washing sheets only at the request of visitors, cutting down on the use of electricity, and so on (Anderen 1993; Wight 1995). However, where this changing focus has become the most noticeable is through the variety of small-scale initiatives that have developed in urban (bed-and-breakfasts), rural (farm tourism) and back-country (ecotourism developments) settings.

Sustainable Design and Ecolodges

Over the past few years, several documents have emerged that analyse the development of ecolodges and ecotourism facilities on the basis of principles of sustainability. However, there appears to be some confusion on the scale and magnitude of development of such areas according to Epler Wood, who reports that ecotourism continues to be misunderstood in resort advertising schemes, while the term 'ecoresort' has yet to be appropriately defined (Shundich 1996). For instance, a tourism industry trade publication recently wrote that 'Another recent and perhaps surprising region for ecoresort development in India. . . . There is interest in genuine cultural experiences within the country. One man has proposed a historical tour of India by rail'.

Interest in sustainable ecotourism design took flight in the early 1990s in part as a result of a US national park service publication dedicated to the principles of sustainable design. Two events took place in the United States that prompted the development of this book. The first was the National Park Service Vail Symposium on October 1991 which discussed, among other things, the severity of environmental stresses within parks; while the second was the Virgin Islands National Park initiative in November 1991, which specifically dealt with issues related to sustainable design in parks and protected areas (US Department of the Interior 1993). The latter publication explores interpretation, natural and cultural resources, site design, building design, energy management, water supply, waste prevention, and facility and maintenance operations in its overview of sustainable design. Of particular importance is its extensive checklist for sustainable building design that emphasises and respects the many interrelationships of all parts of the natural and cultural aspects of the site. However, these were not the first attempts to integrate the developments of humankind with the natural world (especially parks), as evident in the seminal work of Miller (1976, 1989) on ecodevelopment.

Although the US Department of the Interior book is devoted to facility design and construction *in parks,* there is a more generic section that deals specifically with sustainable tourism development. Here the authors advocate using the principles of Aesculapia, which is the Greek place of healing. From this perspective, 'nature is respected for its restorative qualities. The human experience is set in harmony with the environment, and an opportunity is created to allow a reconnection of human needs to the natural systems on which all life is based' (US Department of the Interior 1993: 58). This type of design principle would then strive to meet the following criteria, according to the authors:

(1) provide education for visitors on wildlife, native cultural resources, historic features, or natural features;

(2) involve indigenous populations in operations and interpretation to foster local pride and visitor exposure to traditional values and techniques;

(3) accomplish environmental restoration;

(4) provide research and development on, and/or demonstration projects of, ways to minimise human impacts on the environment;

(5) provide spiritual or emotional recuperation;

(6) provide relaxation and recreation; and

(7) educate visitors to realise that knowledge of our local and global environment is valuable and will empower their ability to make informed decisions.

Russell *et. al.* (1995 : x) define an ecolodge as 'a nature-dependent tourist lodge that meets the philosophy and principles of ecotourism'. Although they underscore the importance of the ecolodge concept from an educational and experiential perspective, they suggest that it is the philosophical time with ecological sensitivity that must define these operations. The importance of ecology is also underscored by the Ecotourism Society, which feels that such lodges promote an educational and participatory experience while at the same time being developed and managed in regard to the local environment in which it exists (Epler Wood in Shundich 1996). Russell *et al.* distinguish between traditional lodges and ecolodges using the 12 points shown in Table 5.2. They further distinguish between the ecolodge and the nature-based lodge, with the latter being associated with fishing, skiing and luxury retreats.

The philosophical issue related to ecolodges identified above is one considered by Andersen (1993, 1994), who feels that along with environmental codes of ethics, a low-impact approach to the design of ecotourism facilities needs to be employed for such facilities to be truly sustainable–an approach that he suggests would entail a complete reworking of the conventional design of architects. Anderson's work is well publicised in the field of ecotourism, especially his advocacy of a number of principles which, broadly defined, include organisational issues (e.g. has an analysis been done of the area's ecological sensitivity?), site planning issues (e.g. minimise trail crossing points at rivers and streams), building design issues (e.g. maintenance of the ecosystem should take priority over view or dramatic design statements), energy resource and utility infrastructure issues (e.g. consider the use of passive or active solar or wind energy sources wherever practical), waste management issues (e.g. provide

Table 5.2
Traditional Lodge *versus* Ecolodge

Traditional	*Ecolodge*
Luxury	Comfortable basic needs
Generic style	Unique character style
Relaxation focus	Activity/educational focus
Activities are facility based (e.g. golf, tennis)	Activities are nature based (e.g. hiking, diving)
Enclave development	Integrated development with local environment
Group/consortium ownership common	Individual ownership common
Profit maximisation based on high guest capacity, services, prices	Profit maximisation based on strategic design, location, low capacity, services, price
High investment	Moderate/low investment
Key attractions are facility and surroundings	Key attractions are surroundings and facility
Gourmet meals, service and presentation	Good/hearty meals and service-cultural influence
Market within chain	Market normally independent
Guides and nature interpreters non-existent or minor feature of operation	Guides and nature interpreters focus of operation

Source : Russell *et al.* (1995).

facilities for recycling), and evaluation (e.g. whether accommodation is made for older guests and physically disabled individuals). Andersen has been able to operationalise many of these design features in his Lapa Rios Resort development on the Osa Peninsula of Costa Rica's Pacific coast. This development has a main lodge in addition to 14 private bungalows which were built by local engineers with the removal of only one tree. (See also Hadley and Grow, 1995, Gurung, 1995 and Wight, 1995 for good discussions on the guidelines and requirements for the design of ecotourism facilities.)

Given the low-capacity and low-impact philosophies of ecotourism development, a logical question is: at what scale does the ecolodge model *not* apply? That is, when is a development considered too big? This question, at least peripherally, has been addressed by Ayala (1996). As an international ecoresort developer, she believes both that ecotourism is becoming a segment of mass tourism, and that it is not incompatible with beach tourism. She supports this view by suggesting that there is the need to diversify the vast number of sea, sun and sand products through the addition of ecotourism (but not at the exclusion of other hard-path experiences). Ayala feels that the line between ecotourists and conventional tourists is least detectable in long-haul travel, citing similarities in their levels of education, household income, and their occupations. Interesting is the fact that (1) the ability to travel long distances is directly related to one's wealth, and (2) wealth is directly related to education and occupation. Ayala fails to discuss other factors (e.g. Psychographics) that determine differences in travel types. For example, the assumption being made is either that all long-haul tourists are ecotourists, or that all ecotourists are simply long-haul travellers. Ayala further writes that many of the mega-resort chains in Africa and Central America go so far as to donate money to conservation efforts. However, if the link is being made to ecotourism, which is the focus of her article, then one wonders what percentage of the revenue from the hotels stays within the local communities and what percentage flows back to North America or Europe. Could such an initiative by the big companies be an appeasement mechanism or marketing scheme designed to look green? (See also the work of Thomlinson and Getz (1996) on scale in ecotourism development.)

It is not easy being sceptical about published work in this area, but increasingly scepticism is what is needed to address some of the issues related to the philosophy and implementation of ecotourism, especially as they relate to ecoresorts. Will Ecotourism's fall from grace be directly attributable to the belief and practice that it fits very nicely as a form of mass tourism, and that mega- ecoresorts are the solution to bring ecotourism to the masses? Is this the rationale for their development–the intrinsic need to not deny the masses their place in the sun (or rather rainforest)? Or rather is it simply that from an extrinsic motivational perspective, it is big business making money the old-fashioned way? Having seen some of these developments first hand, one merely has to dig a bit more closely at some of the unsustainable features of the development. For example, an ecolodge in Mexico recently developed by a large international company used grass and other materials not indigenous to the area in the design of the facility. In addition, no interpretive programmes had been developed to enable tourists to learn about or experience the natural and cultural attractions of the area. Such developments are merely cosmetic, often with few educational and sustainable features, which presumably are important to this segment, and undermine what Hawkins (1994) and others have suggested about ecotourism as being minimum density and low impact. Even in cases where ownership is in the hands of one or a handful of individuals, local ownership is rare.

Ecolodge Research

As outlined earlier in this chapter, ecotourism and the ecolodge concept have been misused by resort advertisers in the past. For this reason research needs to play a stronger role in providing leadership in this area. The following few examples serve to illustrate some of what exists in the area of ecolodge research.

Russell *at al.* (1995) undertook an international ecolodge survey of 28 operators in nine regions around the world (Belize, Costa Rica, Peru, Brazil, Ecuador, the State of Alaska, Australia, New Zealand and Africa). This study discovered that many of the lodges were found in or adjacent to protected areas, with outstanding natural beauty acting as a key to success of the operation. Most of the ecolodges sampled were small in size, accommodating about 24 guests, with some successful operations

CASE STUDY 5.2

Greylock Glen Ecotourism Resort

This recently approved project is a consortium of state, local, not-for-profit agencies, and private interests which have come together to build a demonstration site for the concept of sustainable development in the region of the Berkshire Mountains region of Massachusetts. The developers hope that this site will be a prototype for similar developments throughout the world. (Grand opening is in the year 2000). The resort will operationalise the concepts of sustainable development in offering educational, recreational, and conference-oriented programmes. In particular, visitors will be able to enjoy a golf course (developed from the Audubon Society's guidelines for environmentally sensitive golf courses), a nature centre (a year-round environmental education facility), hiking, Nordic skiing, biking, camping, tennis, swimming, horseback riding, and other recreational activities. In addition to a 200-room resort, 8000 acres will be designated as open, recreational land. The developers (Greylock Management Associates) have specified that the following approaches to sustainability will be followed:

Natural resources :	The maintenance of forest integrity and animal preservation will guide all development decisions at Greylock; a natural resource inventory will be compiled.
Cultural resources:	All cultural artefacts (e.g. farming fields, old roads, orchards) will be preserved and highlighted.
Energy management :	Energy meters will be present and interpret energy usage at the centre.
Water and sewerage :	Water-efficient toilets and shower heads will be used. Visitors will be presented with guidelines to help them cut down on water consumption.
Waste management :	A recycling programme will be implemented, in addition to composing.

in Amazonia catering up to 100 guests. Prices for accommodation (single night), meals and local transportation were approximately US $130–170. The authors felt that although most of the ownership had been typically small scale and independent, corporate ownership was becoming more common. They cited the P&O line in Australia and the Hilton in Kenya as two examples of this recent phenomenon. Finally, they suggested that very few such lodges exist in North America owing to the existing reliance on camping and other, more comfortable recreational lodges. This finding is supported in a recent market study of ecotourism in Alberta and British Columbia (ARA Consultants 1994). However, according to Wight (1995), this is not necessarily what is happening. She feels that market research does not indicate that such a trend is due to market preference, but rather it is due to the demand for a range of accommodation. To Wight, a better question would be to ascertain the range of accommodation types supplied by the region or destination area, where, she feels, there is an abundance of the conventional hotel/motel opportunities. She does, however, feel that there is a distinct lack of adventure-type, small-scale, fixed-roof accommodation (see Fig. 5.2).

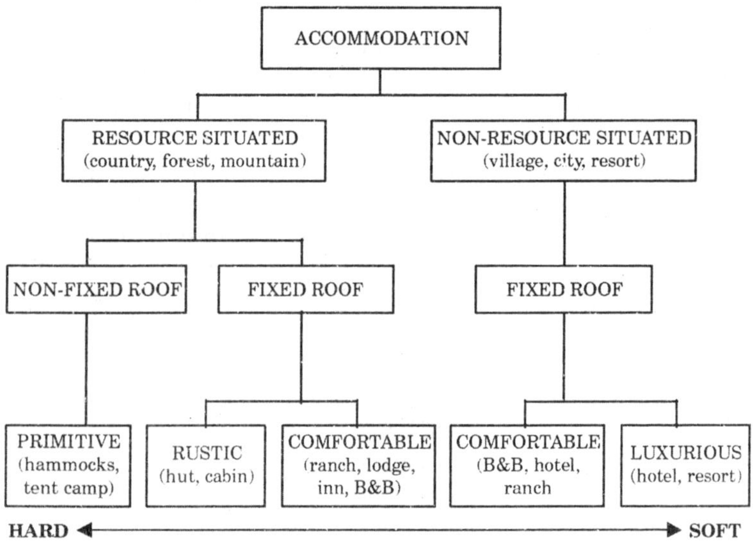

Fig. 5.2. : Ecotourism accommodation spectrum.

The hard aspects of ecotourism can be identified, at least in part, by non-permanent types of dwellings, including tents and hammocks. The ecotourism experience grows continually softer through fixed-roof units (cabins and lodges) on-site, and through fixed-roof dwellings off-site, usually in the form of hostels, hotels and resorts. This hard-soft accommodation continuum relates in part to the work of Laarman and Durst (1987), at least in part, who suggested that one of the hard and soft dimensions of ecotourism was the physical rigour of the trip (see Chapter 2). Those who were prepared to walk extensively in back-country regions, sleep in camps or crude shelters, or tolerate poorer sanitary conditions were said to have been interested in more of a hard-path ecotourism experience.

If this continuum is to apply to North America, it is logical to ask whether or not such operations are applicable to consumptive or non-consumptive forms of recreation. This issue has not been adequately addressed in the literature, at least from the Canadian perspective, and is an issue that is of the utmost importance as outfitters and operators wrestle with how to refit their enterprises to accommodate the changing recreational focus in the north, because, as Anderson/Fast (1996a: 5–4) suggest, 'depending on the characteristics of the package and the participating tourists, outfitter camps [the only form of accommodation in many remote regions of Canada's north] may or may not be appropriate'.

Finally, literature on ecoresorts seems to indicate that accommodation, although important, is not the overriding motivation for visiting regions ARA (1994), for example, places accommodation below the natural setting and wildlife viewing (of primary importance), and other secondary activities related to the experience. To this, Wight (1995) adds support by suggesting that accommodation is an enabler of the overall ecotourism experience; basically tourists select the experience, them choose the accommodation. Often, though, prearranged package tours dictate much of the on-site experience, including choice of accommodation, restricting the opportunity for ecotourists to choose lodging, and reinforcing the point that there is an element of ambiguity as to just what ecotourism entails: According to Grenier *et al.* (1993: 9), 'one person's ecotourism dream may be another's touristic nightmare'.

CONCLUSION

One of the unfortunate realities of ecotourism is that despite its altruistic intentions, to date there is little evidence that it is less intrusive than other types of tourism development. It is indeed frustrating that we continue to talk of appropriate means by which to control development, yet have very few successes to report on. Those who do report success have perhaps not been operating long enough to let, for instance, the destination life cycle unfold.

In many localities around the world, local initiatives are chipping away at the conditions or circumstances that continue to plague ecotourism development. It is within the local arena that such change must occur.

There does seem to be pressure from international development firms to integrate the concept of ecotourism at a grander scale. While there certainly appears to be the opportunity to provide the tourist with a degree of the ecotourism experience at such a scale, caution needs to be used in promoting such areas as true ecotourism sites. Where this relationship between mass tourism resorts and ecotourism breaks down seems to be in relation to the elements of ownership and control at the destination, with international or multinational domination of the industry still in existence. Regions intent on the development of ecotourism must be able to secure both consensus within the community and the means, i.e. the decision-making responsibilities, to move away from many of the conventional global tourism development dysfunctions that are so prevalent within the industry.

6

Ethics and Ecotourism

Grub First : then Ethics–Brecht

In the words above, Brecht strikes to the heart of the dilemma facing ecotourism in many regions of the world today. One cannot help but relate the sentiments of Brecht to Maslow's (1954) hierarchy of needs: simply that people will be moved to satisfy lower-order needs first (those which are physiological, including food, shelter and safety) before upper-level, or psychological, ones (leisure, self-respect and self-actualisation). The implications of Maslow's model to human behaviour are suggestive of the fact that humans are often caught in a duality between what is universally right and personally satisfying or rewarding. It is perhaps why people continue to practise slash-and-burn agriculture; why governments are reluctant to explore other forms of energy use beyond fossil fuels; and why tourist operators are prone to placing more people on sensitive environments than they are supposed to. There appear to be two main motivations for this action along a broad continuum. At one end of the continuum is the need to survive and support a family, while at the other is the need to prosper economically at all costs.

The activities of people are largely normative; that is, collectively they dictate the actions of communities, cultures, societies and the plant. These actions are not always universally right. Indeed, we are now more than ever confronted with a fundamental shift of what constitutes acceptable and unacceptable global behaviour. This has manifested itself in the recent call for governments to reduce greenhouse gas emissions for the purpose of stemming the tide of impending ecological disaster at the hands of global warming and a diminishing ozone layer. Too often, though, the impetus for such action comes only when we are on the brink of major ecological transformations.

According to the theory of reasoned action (Bright *et al.* 1993), we can alter behaviour not from the examination of the attitudes people hold towards certain things—how people respond when asked about their feelings towards one thing or another–but rather through attacking the deep-seated values and beliefs that people hold to be true. In the case of the forerunning examples, we must examine whether people *believe* more strongly in the profit motive or in the preservation of the planet. These beliefs, according to the model, are founded upon the relationship between antecedents (the socialisation of the individual–parents, peers, siblings, etc.) and previous life experiences. Changing people's attitudes and approach to life, or tourism, or commerce, is therefore a difficult process.

Ethics

The application of ethical theory to the realm of business received more attention in the mid-1970s when the first conference on business ethics was organised at the University of Kansas (Bowie 1986). Studies in this area intensified as a result of a number of business-related ethical transgressions, including the abuse of power and business scandals (Sims 1991) at local, regional, national and international scales. Consequently, applied ethics has evolved both in business and in society as a whole to include a number of key areas related to human well-being and development, including business, the legal and medical professions, the biosphere and environment, and, accordingly, tourism, (see Fig. 6.1). Academics have long been involved in philosophical debate over the ethical nature of humankind, and it is from here that the applied side has been able to act on such transgressions. It appears that in ethics, like other disciplines, there is some polarisation with respect to the utility of applied ethics within society, which relates to the perceived role that theory can play in helping to shape application, and also how its application can help drive theory. This dilemma is reinforced by Fox and DeMarco (1986 : 17), who write that:

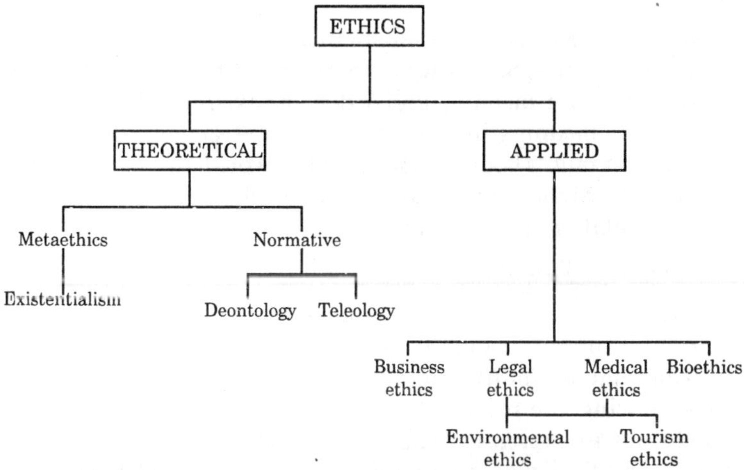

Fig. 6.1 : A framework of moral philosophy.

> Work in applied fields cannot wait for theory to advance to the point of providing clear guidance. Indeed, theory will probably not advance significantly unless current investigations into practical issues reveal areas of agreement and principles on which philosophers can rely in reconstructing their theories.

In the same edited compendium, Singer (1986 : 284) reinforces the relevance of applied ethics as having more of an impact in the field, with theoretical ethics increasingly viewed as having value only in so far it can throw light on the problems of applied ethics.

From the theoretical side, research has tended to emphasise both metaethics (existentialism) and normative ethics (deontology and teleology), with the latter being more prominent by virtue of the fact that it deals with the behaviour of businesses, institutions, and so on. By contrast, existentialism advocates a distinctly individualistic mode of thinking, focusing on the subjective and personal dimensions of human life. Existentialists concern themselves with the question of the nature of being in understanding human existence. Using the example of geography, Tuan (1971) wrote that geographers establish contact with the world in two ways: nomothetically (environmentalism) and ideographically (existentialism). Environmentalism operates in a world of objects, existentialism in a world of purposeful beings. Whereas it is the goal of the environmentalist to search for general laws to discover meaning and order, the existentialist inherently strives for meaning in the landscape 'by tracing man-nature to its basis in man's bodily relation to the world' (*ibid.*: 185). (More on the ethical theories of deontology, teleology and existentialism, as they relate to tourism, follows.)

Ethics and Tourism

Researchers have for some time been instrumental in drawing attention to the various social, ecological and economic impacts of tourism in many regions of the world. Those regions experiencing the most pressure from tourism have been most vociferous in expressing their disdain of the tourism industry's presence. This was never more frankly implied than in the following statement by a Hawaiian delegate of a tourism conference: 'We don't want tourism. We don't want you. We don't want to be degraded as servants and dancers. That is cultural prostitution. I don't want to see a single one of you in Hawaii. There are no innocent tourists' (Pfafflin 1987 : 578). Although this is an example of a social impact or tourism, more fundamentally it is a socially oriented ethical issue. We call attention to issues of this nature because we understand that there has been an injustice to either someone or a group of people. In the case of Hawaii, tourism is an economic cornerstone of the Hawaiian economy. To some people, its presence has contributed significantly to cultural dislocation within the region. Clearly, though, this is not the predominant sentiment that exists within Hawaii, especially from the perspective of those who stand to gain most from the industry. It is those who are realising the economic benefits of the industry who are in most cases supportive of its existence. For example, aboriginal people in Canada have started to come to realise the value of the tourism industry as a vehicle for economic development in their communities, where once they had been more sceptical. In many cases, their scepticism was founded upon the fact that they were not 'players' within the industry, and were therefore no realising any of the potential economic benefits that accrue from the industry.

The presence or absence of acceptable ethical behaviour in tourism settings is very much a function of how tourists, operators, and local people act and feel about each other and towards the resource base. There is the feeling among researchers that a balance must be struck between the various stakeholders of the tourism industry in ensuring that the goodwill of some stakeholders, e.g. tourists and local people, is not overridden by the misgivings of other stockholder groups, e.g. government or industry. The three examples in Case Study 6.1 serve to illustrate this point.

CASE STUDY 6.1

Ethics in Question : Operators, Local People and Tourists

On a recent trip to the jungles of the Yucatán Peninsula in Mexico, our group was taken to a farmer's residence before venturing off to see some of the famous Mayan ruins. At this farm the operator took great joy in showing us three jaguars that were secured to a fence using four-foot chains. The operator's rationale for showing us the jaguars was that he was certain that we would be unable to see jaguars in the forest over the course of our tour. He knew that such a sighting would be highly valued by ecotourists. This was his way of guaranteeing that we saw these magnificent beasts. Clearly, the animals did not mean anything to the operator, and he was taken back by the suggestion of one of our party that he would have rather seen a picture of a jaguar in a book than a live animal under these circumstances.

The second example involves the interference of local people in an ecotourist setting. While in Costa Rica on an eco-tour some ten years ago, we had the pleasure, at a comfortable distance, of witnessing a green sea-turtle laying her eggs one night on a beach. After finishing her task the began to return to the sea, when suddenly a local man appeared and jumped on her back as she made her way. The utilitarian value that he placed on the turtle was clearly one that reflected the sentiment of Costa Rican people at the time, one that is not at all consistent with that of ecotourists. Turtles and turtle eggs are highly prized as a source of food by local people, even though many signs had been put up clearly stating that the personal consumption of turtle eggs was against the law (owing to declining stock).

The final example involves tourists visiting the great Ayers Rock of central Australia. A well-visited attraction, Ayers Rock attracts many different kinds of tourists over the course of the year. While upon Ayers Rock, again some ten years ago, I witnessed two tourists in their early twenties chip away pieces of this monolith as souvenirs to take home. It led me to wonder what the implications of this behaviour would be if all tourists had done the same. It would not take long for such effects to become highly noticeable.

In many cases it is the non-human members of our ecological community that are hardest hit by tourism. For example, in the game reserves in Africa a simple telephone call can organise 50 Land Rovers to converge on a pride of lions in a matter of minutes. It raises the question of equity in a holistic sense, which relates back to the discussion of human domination of the world set out early in this book. Should not all the planet's species have the opportunity to live in an untrammelled, unencumbered, natural state? This may very well be an impractical question, but one nevertheless which needs to be addressed (and is addressed in some of the more radical environmental philosophies such as Deep Ecology and ecofeminism). Myers (1980) illustrates that most people are concerned about issues like the disappearance of species, but not necessarily at the expense of other, more pressing matters such as population and pollution. Similarly, Elliot (1991) writes that there are degrees of environmental ethics to which people submit. These range in philosophy from human-centred ethics, which advocate a stance whereby ethics are evaluated on the basis of how they affect humans; to ecological holism, where the biosphere and the major ecosystems of the planet are morally considerable. Plants, animals, rocks, etc. matter only inasmuch as the maintain the significant whole. Other intermediary ethical stances include animal-centred ethics, where individual members of a species are the focus; life-centred ethics, where all living things are valued (but not necessarily equally); and ethics which imply that all living and non-living things have intrinsic value. Unfortunately, given the fact that tourists cross international, and hence cultural, borders, people do not always evolve an acceptable value-set in relation to the travel destination. This presents itself as a significant dilemma when one considers the adage: when in Rome, do as the Romans do—provided that what the Romans are doing is right (ethical relativism). One wonders whether there exists a more broad-based set of ethical values that ought to apply in all universal situations. This is a key issue that must be addressed in the tourism industry.

In the debate that has raged over the place of mankind on the planet, researchers have come to identify two main opposing paradigms. The first, anthropocentrism, is more of a dominant 'Western' worldview, while the second, biocentrism, is more of a minority, harmonious worldview. The anthopocentric paradigm posits that nature can be conceived only from the perspective of human values. Huankind, therefore, determines the form and function of nature within human society. Conversely, the biocentric philosophy considers that all things in the biosphere have an equal right to exist, i.e. they are all equal in intrinsic value (Deyall and Sessions 1985). In the realm of parks and protected areas, Swinnerton in Philipson (1995) writes that resource managers and other decision-makers around the world

'On three, Vince. Ready?'

Fig. 6.2. : Ethics and African game reserves.

have taken competing views on the place of environmental management in parks. Such views range from preservation to conservation to exploitation, and demonstrate the inconsistency in use of these terms (Fig. 6.3). Those managers advocating the preservationist viewpoint adhere to more of a biocentric philosophy through the practice of little intervention, placing high value on natural resources, responsible use and very small numbers of tourists.

	Resource protection		Resource development
	Preservation ↔	Conservation ↔	Exploitation
View of resource	Biocentric/ anthropocentric	Anthropocentric	Anthropocentric
Level of intervention	No intervention	Limited intervention	Unlimited intervention
Measures of natural value	Undisturbedness Naturalness Completeness	Biodiversity Rareness	
Land use strategy	Segregation	Combination	Segregation/ combination
Access regultions	No use Responsible use Very small numbers	Controlled use Responsible use Small numbers	Unlimited use Abusive use Big numbers Mass tourism

Fig. 6.3 : Characteristics of resource protection and development.

There does appear to be a swaying of public sentiment in favour of a more environmentally oriented ethic according to Philipsen (1995). In citing the work of many authors (Dunlap and Heffernan 1975; Pinhey and Grimes 1979; van Liere and Noe 1981), Philipsen feels that the choices people make with respect to tourism reflect the importance of a environmental values in their live. Urry (1992), for example, writes that the collective tourist 'gaze' of the mass tourism phenomenon seems to be declining in the face of a more romantic gaze exemplified through green tourism.

Too Little Research

Fundamentally, there is a very weak foundation of research in tourism ethics studies to date (D'Amore 1993; Payne and Dimanche 1996). There does however appear to be growing recognition within tourism's public, private and not-for-profit sectors that, from the perspective of sustainable development, ethical concerns have not fallen upon deaf ears. According to Hughes (1995), it is only the technical, rational and scientific province of sustainability that has predominated to date, rather than the ethical province which was most responsible for the initial drive for a newer and more holistic development paradigm.

In the past, tourism ethics has been relegated to the area of hospitality management owing to the emphasis of hospitality's relationship to service and business (Wheeler 1994). This research provided the foundation for the move to establish the International Institute for Quality and Ethics in Service and Tourism (IIQUEST), which was designed to bridge the gap between ethics and issues related to community relations, sexual harassment, the rights of guests, and so on (see Hall 1993). However, the Rio Earth summit of 1992 was a principal catalyst in generating more interest in the utility of ethics in the realm of tourism research—especially codes of ethics—where those in attendance committed themselves to Agenda 21. Genot (1995 : 166) outlines chapter 30 of this plan :

> Business and Industry, including transnational corporations, should be encouraged to adopt and report on the implementation of codes of conduct promoting best environmental practice, such as the International Chamber of Commerce's Business Charter on Sustainable Development and the chemical industry's responsible care initiative.

Recently, a number of articles have surfaced either in response to the dearth of literature on tourism and ethics, and/or as a logical progression in the evolution of tourism research. This recent intensification is indeed timely as tourism researcher grapple with more philosophical issues that relate to business, society and the environment. These additions to the literature include general discussions on ecotourism and ethics (Duenkel and Scott 1994; Kutay 1989), more specific commentary on ecotourism and ethics (Karwacki and Boyd 1995; Wight 1993a), tourism ethical decision-

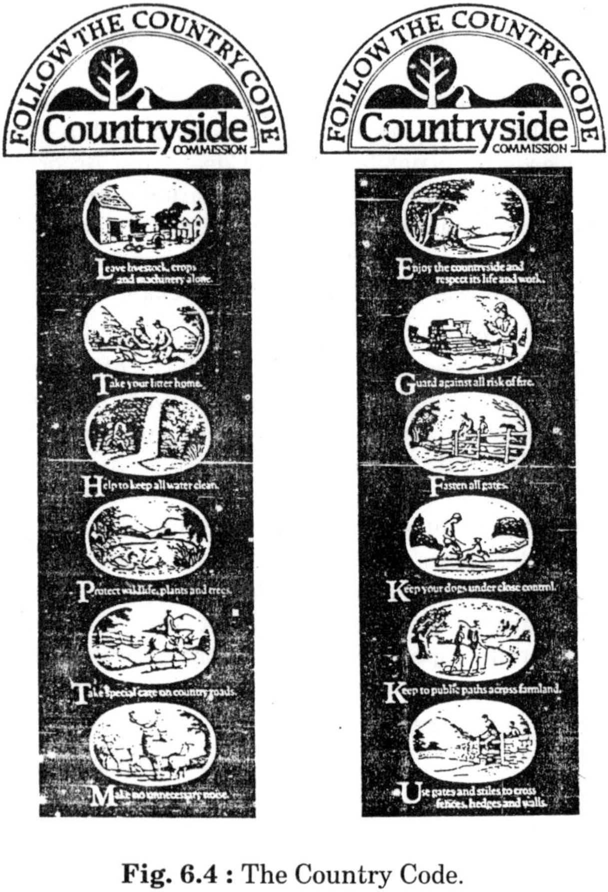

Fig. 6.4 : The Country Code.

making on the quality of life in Third World countries, and ethics and marketing in the ecotourism industry (Wight 1993b).

A recurrent theme in many of the aforementioned publications is the advocacy of codes of conduct/ethics for the tourism industry. The British Columbia Ministry of Development, Industry, and Trade (1991 : 2-1) defines a code of ethics as 'a set of guiding principles which govern the behaviour of the target group in pursuing their activity of interest'. From an industry perspective, they function as 'messages through which corporations hope to shape employee behaviour and effect change through explicit statements of desired behaviour' (Stevens 1994 : 64). In tourism, such codes have gone beyond the realm of business to ensuring that local people, government, and tourists abide by predetermined guidelines. There has been a proliferation of such codes over the past few years by a variety of organisations including governments, NGOs, and industry, many of which can be found in the work by Mason and Mowforth (1995) and the United Nations Environment Programme Industry and Environment (1995). An example of such a guideline is the Country Code, which was one of the first (Figure 6.4).

According to Scace *et al.* (1992) codes fall into two main categories: codes of ethics and codes of practice/conduct. The former, according to the authors, are philosophical and value-based, whereas the latter are more applicable and specific to actual practice in local situations. An example of a guideline falling within a code of ethics would be 'respect the frailty of the earth'; while an example of a code of practice guideline would probably be oriented more towards acceptable business practice with reference to the organisation's 'commitment' to the customer. This dichotomy, though, is somewhat misleading as it implies that codes of practice/conduct are not concerned with values. Although codes of conduct ought to be specific in actual situations, as suggested, they should also be founded upon a sound ethical principle as outlined in the previous discussion on ethics and business.

The link between the tourism industry and ethics has been discussed by Payne and Dimanche (1996 : 997) who suggest that codes of ethics ought to project a number of key values, including justice, integrity, competence, and utility, in illustrating that—

(1) The tourism industry must recognise that its basis is a limited resource, the environment, and that sustainable economic development requires limits to growth.

(2) The tourism industry must realise that it is community-based, and that greater consideration must be given to the socio-cultural costs of tourism development.

(3) The tourism industry must also recognise that it is service oriented, and that it must treat employees as well as customers ethically.

Genot (1995) further underscores the practical reasons for industry to associate itself with codes of conduct, stating that, among other factors, a sound environment means good business, meeting consumer demand, unifying industry efforts and image, and assuring product quality. Genot feels that the following principles are at the core of any code of ethics: environmental commitment, responsibility, integrated planning, environmentally sound management, cooperation between decision-makers and public awareness. Many of these principles are elaborated upon in other publications devoted specifically to the ethical conduct of operators and other members of the tourism industry (see Dowling 1992; and The Ecotourism Society 1993). The Ecotourism Society publication, for example, has developed guidelines for predeparture, guiding, monitoring, management and local accommodations.

Stronger consideration needs to be given to the formation and understanding of these codes, according to Malloy and Fennell (1998). These authors subjected 40 codes (414 individual guidelines) to content analysis on the basis of who guidelines were developed for, who guidelines were developed by, the type of tourism they were directed towards, the orientation of the code, the mood of the message, and the main focus of the guideline. These variables were juxtaposed with two philosophies of ethics (deontology and teleology), in addition to determining whether the codes were relevant to a local ('local' included local, regional and national scales) or cosmopolitan (meaning a universal code) condition. Deontology is an ethical approach which suggests that an act is right or wrong on the basis of rules or principles of action or duties or rights or virtues (Mackie 1977). This approach advocates behaviour that is means-based or intentions-based in its orientation. Deontology, or right behaviour, provides us with guidance through the provision of rules and regulations to follow; is essence, our 'duty' is laid out for us and we 'ought' to adhere to it. For example, tour operators will abide by organisational policies developed for the purpose of honouring established environmental or cultural norms. An example of a deontological code is as follows: be aware of the periphery of a rookery or seal colony, and remain outside it. Follow the instructions given by your leaders. Conversely, teleology, or good behaviour, is an ethical approach which suggests that an act is right or wrong solely on the basis of the consequences of its performance (Brody 1983). Because of its orientation towards the consequences of one's action, it is ends-based. In this sense, the stakeholder is released from following the tradition or dogma of the past and is able to choose in a manner which is consistent with the changing circumstances of societies and cultures. An example of a teleological code is as follows: Do not enter buildings at the research stations unless invited to do so. Remember that scientific research is going on, and *any intrusion could affect the scientists' data.* (The consequence of the action is highlighted in italics.) Figure 6.5 illustrates the methodology employed in the study, for each of the 414 guidelines.

In this research, approximately 77 per cent of all guidelines in the study were found to be deontological in nature. As such these guidelines, according to Malloy and Fennell, fail to provide the decision-maker (e.g. tourist) with the rationale for abiding by a particular code, with the assumption that an explanation of consequence (i.e. the teleological premise) is unnecessary to the tourist or other stakeholer. More specifically, it was found that most of the codes were developed by associations (NGOs), and for tourists; many of the codes were ecologically based rather than socially or economically based; about 85 per cent positively

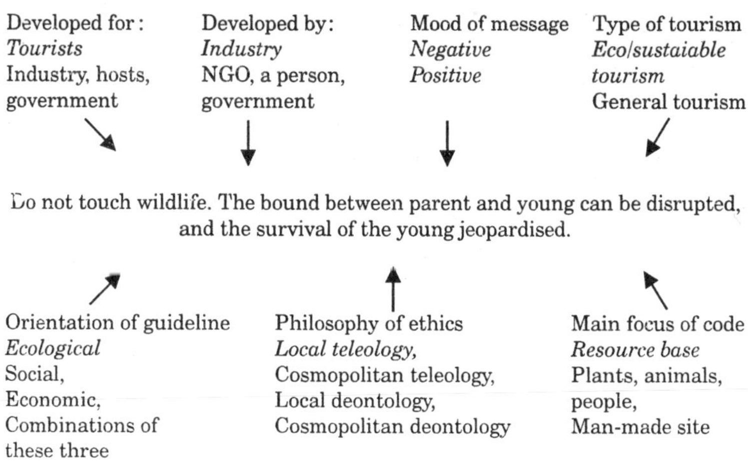

Fig. 6.5. : Example of an Antarctica code of ethics guideline.

stated; and the focus of such codes was on people or the resource base. Malloy and Fennell recommend that future research in the area of codes of ethics should explore the deeper philosophical meaning of codes, advocate more of the teleological perspective in the development of codes, i.e. the consequences of one's action if the code is not adhered to, and should aim at a better understanding of the extent to which codes actually affect or change behaviour.

Despite what appears to be normative acceptance of the utility of codes of ethics in the tourism industry, it is clear that they have not been universally embraced by tourism researchers. Wheeller, for example, is not convinced of their utility, as demonstrated in a stinging review of ecotourism. He feels that there are no answers to the confusion surrounding both ecotourism and sustainable tourism, but simply

> a never-ending series of laughable codes of ethics: codes of ethics for travellers; codes of ethics for tourists, for government, and for tourism businesses. Codes for all—or, more likely, codeine for all. . . .But who really believes these codes are effective? I am pretty wary of platitudinous phrases like 'we are monitoring progress'. Has there been any progress—indeed, has there been any monitoring? Perhaps I am missing it and the answer itself is actually in code.
>
> (Wheeller 1994 : 651)

Beyond Codes of Ethics

As stated earlier, the base of ethics and tourism/ecotourism research is at present quite limited. Given this fact, it is the purpose of this section to highlight some of the work in this area as a means by which to provide a basic understanding of the extent and appropriateness of this work to the future of ecotourism studies.

In a well-prepared essay on ethics and tourism, Hultsman (1995) proposes the use of a framework of ethics and tourism based on the notion of 'just' tourism, which refers not only to acting in a fair, honourable, and proper manner, but also to the fact that tourism is 'merely' or 'only' a 'small thing'. With reference to the latter aspect of the framework, Hultsman emphasises that tourism has become more important as an economy than as an experience, and as such has lost some of its intrinsic qualities that are derived through the pleasure of experience. He notes that 'Should tourism reach the point of being considered by service providers as first a business and second an experience, it is no longer "just tourism"; it is industry' (*ibid.*: 561). He concludes his paper by suggesting that ethical issues need to be included in the textbooks used in tourism curricula, and further that, like many other authors, we ought to be concerned that there is a real lack of professionalism in the delivery of tourism services.

In other related research, Upchurch and Ruhland (1995 : 37) focused on advancing the hospitality industry's understanding of ethical work-climate types through an analysis of the normative ethical theories of Egoism ('an individual should follow the greatest good for oneself'), Benevolence ('actions that are delivered on a fair and impartial basis, are based on maximising the good, and follow impartial distribution rules'), and Principle (which 'is a theory suggesting that decisions are based on rules. The outcome or actions should be based on the merit of the rule'). Respondents were Missouri lodging operators who filled out the Likert-style ethical climate questionnaire designed to measure the three ethical theories. These authors found that Benevolence was the most frequently perceived ethical climate type present in the lodging respondents (which, they say, is consistent with the literature). Benevolence, therefore, indicated a certain responsiveness to the clientele in a socially oriented manner.

This element of social responsibility is also discussed in a paper on business ethics and tourism by Walle (1995). He discusses the dichotomy that exists in business ethics theory as established by the work of Friedman and Davis. He illustrates that for the Friedman school, the *modus operandi* of business is to generate profits, and that it is not the responsibility of business leaders to dwell upon social policies and strategies (within the law). On the other hand, he argues that the Davis school advocates a more socially responsible behaviour for business, which will in turn lead to greater profits and prevent government intervention, through the generation of positive publicity (Table 6.1). Through these extremes, Walle argues that tourism, because of its uniqueness, cannot follow the universal or generic strategies of mainstream business which focus on the organisation and its customers (e.g. manufacturing). Instead, he makes the point that

> Tourism is not a generic industry since it uniquely impacts on the environment, society and cultural systems in ways which require a holistic orientation within a broad and multidimensional context. Contemporary business ethics, however, has been slow to embrace such a holistic perspective. Historically, the focus has been on the organisation and its customers. Impacts on third parties (externality issues) have often been ignored. (Walle 1995 : 226)

His initial conceptualisation on social obligation, responsibility, and responsiveness is reworked to illustrate how such orientations might be applied to tourism's uniqueness (Table 6.2).

In work related more specifically to ecotourism, Fennell and Malloy (1995) drew a relationship between metaethics (existentialism) and normative ethics (deontology and teleology) in discussing how each can contribute to comprehensive ethical decision-making in the ecotourism industry. This, they reason, is a deviation away from the traditional manner by which to resolve ethical decisions, i.e. mediating between the two dichotomous approaches of metaethics and normative ethics.

Existentialism implies that an act is right or wrong according to the actor's free will, responsibility, and authenticity (Guignon 1986). Existentialism or authentic behaviour favours neither ends nor means, but rather the premise that individuals need to be self-aware and prepared to take full responsibility for their actions. In essence, this provides the opportunity for individuals to choose freely their behavioural patterns within the confines of their own acceptance of responsibility for all consequences on all things. Deontology and teleology have been discussed above.

Fennell and Malloy go on to suggest that although each of the three (existentialism, deontology and teleology) advocates radically different perspectives, stakeholders or decision-makers in search of comprehensive ethical decisions may employ any of them to arrive at ethically good, right and authentic solutions. Also, according to these authors, it is not the case that people

Table 6.1
Ethical Orientations : A Comparison

	Social obligation no. 1 (Friedman)	*Social responsibility no. 2 (Davis)*	*Social responsiveness (extension of No. 2)*
General overview	Legal and profitable	Current social problems are responded to	Future social and/or environmental problems are anticipated and addressed
Choosing options	The sole consideration aside from profit is legality	Decisions respond to social issues which overtly need to be addressed	Decisions based on anticipation of future needs and/or social problems even if they do not impact or are caused by the firm
Strategies are evaluated with reference to:	Is the strategy legal? Is the strategy profitable enough?	Has the organisation responded to problems and issues which have emerged as significant?	Future problems are addressed even if the organisation is not directly causing them

Source : Walle 1995.

Table 6.2
Special Ethical Considerations of Tourism

Tourism's perspective	*Social obligation no. 1 (Friedman)*	*Social responsibility no. 2 (Davis)*	*Social responsiveness (extension of No. 2)*
Progress is not inevitable or inherently beneficial	Since the concept of 'progress' is not universal or inevitable, we should not place an over-reliance upon it in our strategies/tactics	Tourism has a responsibility to encourage development which meshes with the local environment and culture, not in accordance with a universal concept of 'progress'	Since 'progress' leads to concomitant changes in culture and the environment, tourism strategy should be appropriate and mitigate its impact
Tourism can be undermined by pressures of the industry	Change wrought by tourism might undercut the industry. Such potential should be prevented and mitigated when doing so is a good tactic.	Tourism causes negative impacts and pressures on people and the environment which should be mitigated	The industry has both practical and ethical reasons to respond to impacts on the environment and local people
All relevant stakeholders need to be considered when strategies are forged	Government regulation and loan conditions might demand responding to the needs of all relevant stakeholders	Tourism should respond to the needs of various stakeholders which are impacted on by the industry	The industry should anticipate future impacts from various sources and respond in proactive ways

Source : Walle 1995.

rely exclusively on one pure form of ethics as a means by which to make decisions. They feel that what might be termed a triangulated approach would correspond to the many demands, both organisational and moral, that exist within the tourism industry (Figure 6.6). For the ecotourist, this would accomplish two things—

> First the individual is provided with an ethical criteria [*sic*] with which to assess and resolve issues in a comprehensive fashion that is normative as well as introspective. As a result, it is hoped that what for many may be a latent sense of ethics, may become more apparent and considered as a result of exploring teleological, deontological and existential perspectives. A second consequence of this model is that it is used as a point of departure for not only empirical research of the behaviour of ecotourists, but also for the development of more comprehensive ethical conduct for the ecotourism industry in general (e.g. organisational culture, climate).
>
> (Fennell and Malloy 1995 : 178)

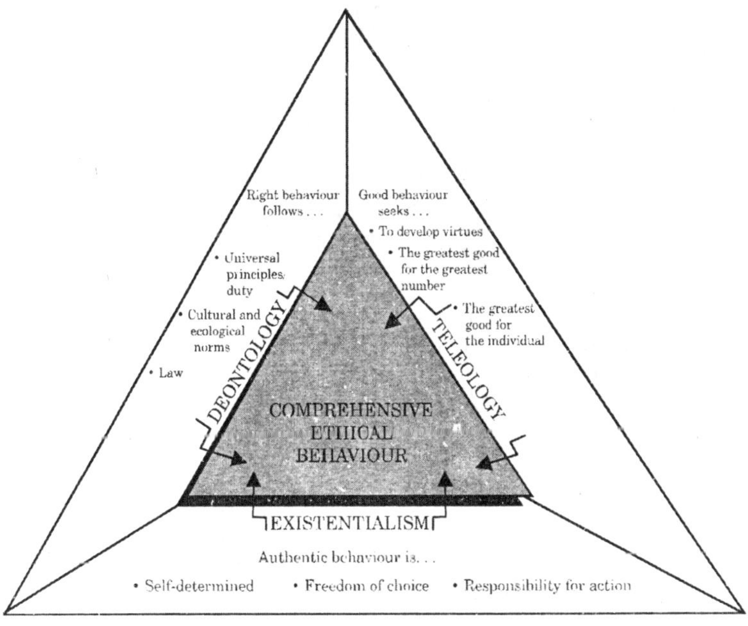

Fig. 6.6 : A Model of Ethical Triangulation.

In other research, Malloy and Fennell (1998) examined the organisational culture literature in attempting to differentiate between ethical and non-ethical work climates in the ecotourism industry (Figure 6.7), on the basis of work by Schein (1985) and Kohlberg (1981, 1984). Schein wrote that culture sets certain standards of acceptable behaviour within an organisation. Individuals are thereby subject to a process of socialisation based on normative and value-based behaviours of the organisation. On the other hand, Kohlberg's work is fundamental to our

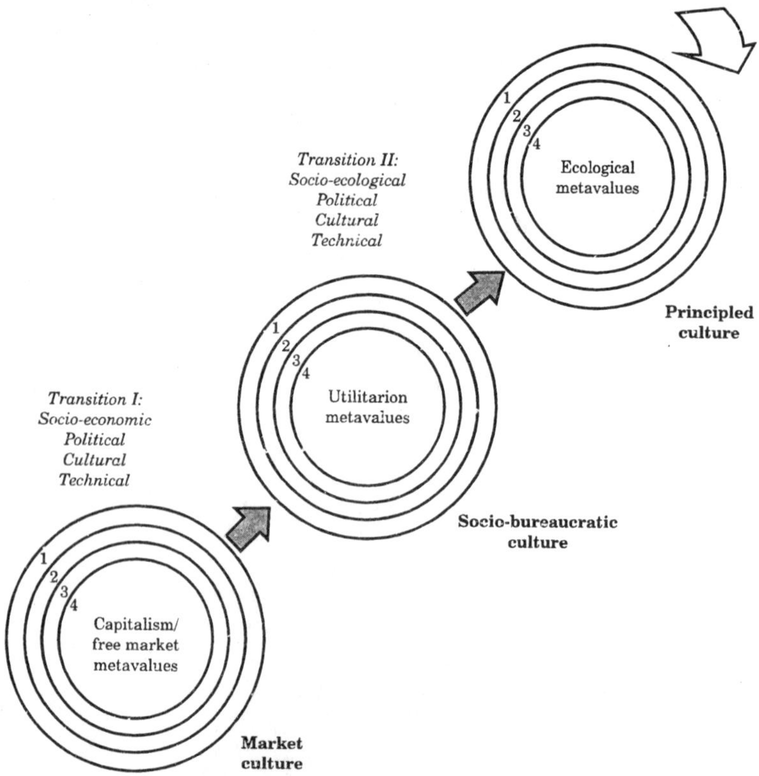

Fig. 6.7. : Moral development in ecotourism organisational cultures. (1) Artefacts of the ecotourism organisation; (2) patterns of individual behaviour in the ecotourism organisation; (3) values and beliefs of the ecotourism organisation; (4) basic assumptions of the ecotourism organisation.

understanding of moral development within society from the perspective of three distinct phases: pre-conventional (people who act to avoid punishment, receive rewards from external sources, seek pleasure, and give little consideration to social norms and ecological principles); conventional (individuals act to gain approval within society by adhering to social sanctions); and post-conventional (defined by the move to be influenced not by external forces, but rather from within for the good of the community, but also, more broadly, for the good of humanity and the planet). Malloy and Fennell termed these three phases, applied to ecotourism, respectively: (1) the market ecotourism culture, (2) the socio-bureaucratic ecotourism culture, and (3) principled ecotourism culture. According to these authors, it is this last stage that the ecotourism industry must strive to reach, which demands not solely an economic and/or sociological agenda, but rather a socioecological change that reflects the general goals of ecological and social holish. The transitions between stages are influenced by broad political processes (e.g. the development of policies to control tourism impacts); cultural processes (e.g. promotion within firms based on socially and ecologically responsible behaviour); and technical processes (e.g. certification of ecotourism guides).

CONCLUSION

One of the concerns that many people in the field of ecotourism share, at least from the research standpoint, is the lack of empirical data to substantiate many of the claims being made about ecotourism as being more responsible than other forms of tourism. For example, is ecotourism a greener form of tourism than other forms? Are ecotourists more ethically based than other types of tourists? What about their values and attitudes? These and other questions must be addressed in order to profile this type of tourism more accurately. A potentially fruitful area in differentiating ecotourists from other types of tourists is through an analysis of values. Conventional measures used in other social science fields include Rokeach's Value Survey, the Values and Lifestyle Scale, and the List of Values Scale (see Madrigal and Kahle 1994; and Kahle *et al.* 1986). Madrigal (1995) writes that owing to their centrality to a person's cognitive structure, personal values, and therefore scales of this nature, are effective predictors of human behaviour. In relation to attitudes, the New Environmental Paradigm (NEP) scale has been moderately successful at measuring beliefs about humankind's dominance and harmony with the natural world (Jurowski *et al.* 1995), and may also lend some support in differentiating between, for example, ecotourists and mass tourists within a destination. Finally, in the context of the business literature, Reidenbach and Robin (1988, 1990) have developed a Multidimensional Ethics Scale (MES) which is designed to determine the ethical differences between subjects on the basis of deontological, teleological, justice and relativistic theories of ethics. Using this scale, Fennell and Malloy (1997) found that ecotour operators were moderately more ethical than other types of operators (fishing, cruise line, adventure and golf) on the basis of their responses to three tourism scenarios, providing some empirical evidence to suggest that, at least from the perspective of operators, ecotourism is in fact a more ethically based sector of the tourism industry.

7

Structural Equation Modelling

Introduction

During the last decade structural equation modelling (SEM) has increasingly been applied in the marketing discipline, particularly in the US. In the tourism discipline this technique has not been applied widely. The concept of SEM is difficult to understand due to its statistical complexity and non-user-friendly computer manuals.

This chapter introduces the basic concepts associated with SEM using LISREL in a comprehensive and non-technical manner. It is based upon the article 'Structural equation modelling with LISREL : application in tourism by Y. Reisinger and L. Turner published in *Tourism Management,* Vol. 20, No. 1, 1999, pp. 71-88, reprinted with permission from Elsevier Science. The purpose of this chapter is to: (1) explain the concept of SEM modelling, its major objectives and advantages; (2) show how useful structural models are in solving research problems within the tourism discipline; (3) present the major steps involved in the formulation and testing of a LISREL model through an application of LISREL modelling to test an hypothesis about the relationship between the tourist perceptions of a beach resort and their satisfaction with the resort; and (4) draw attention to potential limitations associated with the LISREL approach.

What is Structural Equaltion Modelling?

Structural equation modelling is a multivariate technique that combines (confirmatory) factor analysis modelling from psychometric theory and structural equations modelling associated with econometrics. The term 'structural' assumes that the parameters reveal a causal relation. However, the technique does not 'discover' causal relations. 'At best, it shows whether the causal assumptions embedded in a model match a sample of data' (Bollen, 1989, p. 4).

Objectives of Structural Equation Modelling

The primary aim of SEM is to explain the pattern of a series of interrelated dependence relationships simultaneously between a set of latent (unobserved) constructs, each measured by one or more manifest (observed) variables.

The measured (observed) variables in SEM have a finite number of values. Examples of measured variables are distance, cost, size, weight or height. The measured (manifest) variables are gathered from respondents through data collection methods, or collected as secondary data from a published source. They are represented by the numeric responses to a rating scale item on a questionnaire. Measure variables in SEM are usually continuous.

On the other hand, latent (unobserved) variables are not directly observed, have an infinite number of values, and are usually continuous. Examples of latent constructs are attitudes, customer satisfaction, and perception of value or quality. Latent variables are theoretical constructs that can be determined to exist only as a combination of other measurable variables. As such they are similar to principal components and are sometimes theoretically justified from a previous factor analysis.

In this primary form of analysis SEM is similar to combining multiple regression and factor analysis. As such, the SEM expresses the linear relationship between two separate sets of latent constructs (which may have been derived by two separate factor analyses). When using SEM these latent constructs are termed exogenous (independent) constructs and endogenous (dependent) constructs. Figure 7.6 shows that endogenous latent constructs such as repeat visitation and satisfaction depend on independent exogenous latent constructs such as culture and perception.

The SEMs include one or more linear regression equations that describe how the endogenous constructs depend upon the exogenous constructs. Their coefficients are called path coefficients or sometimes regression weights.

However, there is an important difference between factor analysis modelling and SEM modelling. In factor analysis the observed variables can load on any and all factors (constructs). The number of factors is constrained. When using SEM confirmatory factor analysis is used and the observed variables are loaded onto particular constructs. The loadings are free or fixed at particular values, and the independence or co-variance of variables is specified.

Although the primary purpose of SEM is the analysis of latent constructs and in particular the analysis of links between latent constructs, SEM is also capable of other forms of analysis. SEM can be used to estimate variance and covariance, test hypotheses, conventional linear regression and factor analysis. In complex analysis frameworks SEM may be preferable to conventional statistical methods, for example, where it is required to test whether factor analysis on data from several populations yields the same factor model simultaneously. Another example is where a multiple regression is required to test for several dependent variables from the same set of independent variables simultaneously, particularly if it is possible for one dependent variable to simultaneously determine another. The SEM is a powerful method for effectively dealing with multicollinearity (when two or more variables are highly correlated), which is one of the benefits of SEM over multiple regression and factor analysis.

All aspects of SEM modelling must be directed by theory, which is critical for model development and modification. A clear misuse of SEM can occur when data is simply fitted to a suitable SEM and theory is then expanded from the analytic result.

There are three components in general structural equation models. (1) Path analysis; (2) the conceptual synthesis of latent variable and measurement models; and (3) general estimation procedures (Bollen, 1989).

Application of Structural Equation Modelling

SEM modelling has been widely used in a number of disciplines, including psychology (Agho *et al.*, 1992; Shen *et al.*, 1995), sociology (Kenny, 1996), economics (Huang, 1991), criminology (Junger, 1992), cross-national (Mullen, 1995; Singh, 1995), cross-cultural research (Riordan and Vandenberg, 1994), healthcare (Babakus and Mangold, 1992; Taylor, 1994a; Taylor and Cronin, 1994), gerontology (Russell, 1990), human resources management (Medsker *et al.*, 1994), environmental studies (Nevitte and Kanji, 1995), family studies (Fu and Heaton, 1995), religious studies (Legge, 1995), migration studies (Sandu and De Jong, 1995), marketing, and many others. In the marketing discipline, LISREL has been used in a variety of applications, including consumer behaviour (Oliver and Swan, 1989; Singh, 1990; Fornell, 1992; Heide and Miner, 1992; Lichtenstein *et al.*, 1993; McCarty and Shrum, 1993; Taylor and Baker, 1994; Spreng *et al.*, 1996), organisational buying behaviour (Michaels *et al.*, 1987), channel management (Schul and Babakus, 1988), product policy (DeBrentani and Droge, 1988), pricing strategy (Walters and MacKenzie, 1988), advertising (MacKenzie and Lutz, 1989), salesforce management (Dubinsky *et al.*, 1986), retailing (Good *et al.*, 1988), international marketing (Han, 1988), services marketing (Arora and Cavusgil, 1985; Crosby *et al.*, 1990; Hui and Bateson, 1991; Francese, 1991; Cronin and Taylor, 1992; Brown *et al.*, 1993; Price *et al.*, 1995; Taylor, 1994b), service quality in retail stores (Dabholkar *et al.*, 1996), and service satisfaction (Jayanti and Jackson, 1991). There are many other examples.

Reasons for Popularity

The reason why SEM modelling has been applied in so many disciplines is its ability to solve research problems related to relationships between latent constructs, which are measured by observed variables. For example, such relationships can be found in educational research where the determinants of educational achievements and failure are analysed, or in consumer behavioural research where the reasons for purchasing various products and services are analysed. Many important marketing, psychological or cultural concepts are latent constructs, with unknown reliability, measured by multiple observed variables. The lower the measurement reliability the more difficult it is to observe relationships between the latent constructs and other variables. By using SEMs one can model important latent constructs while taking into account the unreliability of the indicators. Also, many latent constructs such as perceptions, evaluation, satisfaction, or behaviour measures have low reliability. By using regression one may get coefficients with unexpected signs; the predictors one would expect to be positively related to the dependent variable end up with negative coefficients, or *vice versa*. Regression analysis as opposed to SEM analysis does not eliminate the difficulties caused by unreliable measures. The SEM's consider unknown reliability of the measures and rank the measures in terms of their importance (Bacon *et al.*, 1998).

Application in Tourism

SEM modelling has not been widely used in the tourism discipline, outside the US. However, the application of SEM in tourism is important as a tool for promoting better quality research. Tourism researchers are often faced with a set of interrelated questions. What variables determine tourist arrivals to a particular destination? How does demand as a latent variable combine with supply variables to affect tourist arrivals? How do demand and supply variables simultaneously affect tourist purchasing decisions and holiday satisfaction? How does tourist holiday satisfaction result in repeat visitation and loyalty to a destination? Many of the same independent variables affect different dependent variables with different effects. Other multivariate techniques do not address these questions within a single comprehensive method.

In the tourism discipline structural modelling has recently been used to assess traveller types (Nickerson and Ellis, 1991), hotel guest satisfaction (Gundersen *et al.*, 1996), service quality and satisfaction in the hotel/motel industry (Getty and Thompson, 1994; Thomson and Getty, 1994), tourists' and retailers' perceptions of service levels in a tourism destination (Vogt and Fesenmaier, 1995), factors that influence guest accommodation choice intentions (Richard and Sundaram, 1993), relationship between travel motivation and information sources in the senior travel market (Kim *et al.*, 1996), antecedents of customer expectations of restaurants (Clow *et al.*, 1996), resident attitudes toward tourism (Lindberg and Johnson, 1997), impact of tourism advertising on tourist spending (Butterfield *et al.*, 1998), response to wilderness recreation fees (Williams *et al.*, 1999), influence of tourists' experiences on holiday satisfaction and on the change of attitudes (Jacinto *et al.*, 1999), cultural differences between Asian tourists and Australian hosts (Reisinger and Turner, 1998a, 1999a, b; 2002b), importance and expectations of destination attributes (Turner and Reisinger, 1999), tourism flows from the UK to seven major destinations (Turner *et al.*, 1998), shopping satisfaction (Reisinger and Turner, 2002c; Turner and Reisinger

2001), golf travellers' satisfaction (Petrick and Backman, 2002), and many others.

Gundersen *et al.*, (1996) identified important factors for hotel guest satisfaction among business travellers. The analysis covered three departments of hotel operations (receptions, food and beverage, and house-keeping) and two dimensions of satisfaction (tangible and intangible). The structural model showed the relationships among the three departments and overall satisfaction with the hotel. The highest loadings were noted on the service aspects of all departments. The major explanatory variables for overall hotel guest satisfaction were tangible aspects of housekeeping and intangible aspects of reception service, suggesting that by focusing on these factors, high levels of satisfaction among business travellers can be achieved.

Getty and Thompson (1994) tested customers' perceptions of the lodging sector performance on multiple dimensions and the perceived level of overall quality possessed by the lodging property satisfaction with the lodging experience, and customers' willingness to recommend the property. The customers' intentions to recommend the property were determined by their perceptions of the overall quality of the property, rather than their satisfaction with the stay. The specific quality and satisfaction dimensions, most responsible for willingness to recommend the property, included: the general appearance of the property, perceived value associated with the stay, willingness of employees to listen, and the degree to which the property provided a safe environment. Thompson and Getty (1994) suggested that customers, intentions to provide positive word of mouth are a function of their perceptions of the overall quality of the lodging property, rather than their expressed level of satisfaction with stay.

Vogt and Fesenmaier (1995) used four service quality dimensions (reliability, responsiveness, assurance, accessibility), measured by thirteen items, to evaluate service experiences as perceived by tourists and retailers. The results showed that tourists evaluated services differently to retailers.

Kim *et al.*, (1996) tested a causal relationship between tourism motivation and information sources. They found that the more active travellers in the senior market were more likely to consult information sources before travel. Those who travelled to get rest and relaxation were less likely to search for travel information. Those who travelled to visit friends and families were not interested in searching for travel information.

Lindberg and Johnson (1997) tested two models to assess how the values people hold influence their attitudes toward tourism and what types of outcomes most affect attitudes. The value-attitude model showed that resident values regarding economic gains were better determinants of attitudes than values regarding disruption within the community. The expectancy-value model indicated that perceived economic and congestion impacts had greater influence on attitudes than perceived crime and aesthetic impacts.

Reisinger and Turner (1998a) determined which cultural differences between Asian tourists and Australian hosts are predictors of tourist satisfaction. The results indicated that differences in cultural values and rules of social behaviour between Asian tourists and Australian hosts directly influence tourist satisfaction, and differences in perceptions of service directly influence tourist social interaction. Perceptions of service providers only indirectly determine satisfaction through the mediating effect of interaction.

Turner and Reisinger (1999) determined the relationships between destination attributes importance and Japanese tourist expectations of those attributes on arrival, and confirmed that a study of satisfaction of destination attributes should be based upon a comparison of expectations on arrival against satisfaction on departure.

Reisinger and turner (2002c) tested the theory that shopping satisfaction results from the importance of product attributes, which in turn, depend on the types of products purchased. They showed that the products considered important by Japanese tourists visiting Hawaii determine the importance of attributes and the importance of attributes determine tourist satisfaction.

Petrick and Backman (2002) found that golf travellers' overall satisfaction was determined by information satisfaction and attribute satisfaction. Attributes related to the resort experience had more influence on overall satisfaction than attributes related to information provided and gold experiences.

Types of LISREL Modelling

LISREL stands for Liner Structural Relationships and is a computer programme for covariance structure analysis. It was originally introduced by Joreskog and Van Thiilo in 1972.

The general LISREL model has many sub-models as special cases. The mathematical notations are presented on the following page, followed by a presentation of the different sub-models.

Abbreviations

x – measured independent variable

y – measured dependent variable

ξ – latent exogenous construct explained by x-variables

η – latent endogenous construct explained by y-variables

δ – error for x-variable

ε – error for y-variable

λ – correlation between measured variables and all latent constructs

γ – correlation between latent constructs ξ (exogenous) and η (endogenous)

ϕ – correlation between exogenous latent constructs ξ

β – correlation between endogenous latent constructs η.

Submodel 1 is the LISREL model, which is designed to measure observed variables. The model has only x, ξ, and δ-error variables. There are no y- and η-variables (see abbreviations). The data used measures only the correlation between the constructs (see Figure 7.1).

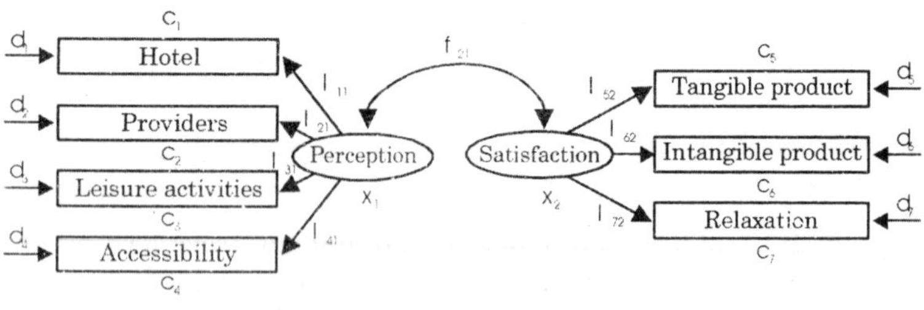

Fig. 7.1 : Hypothetical model: submodel 1.

Submodel 2 is the LISREL model, which is designed to estimate relationships among directly measured independent variables and the dependent variable(s). The model has no latent variables but there are two kinds of directly measured variables: x, y, and ζ-error variables. There are four types of LISREL Submodel 2: a single regression model, bivariate model, recursive model, and non-recursive model. The examples of these models are graphically presented in Figure 7.2-7.5.

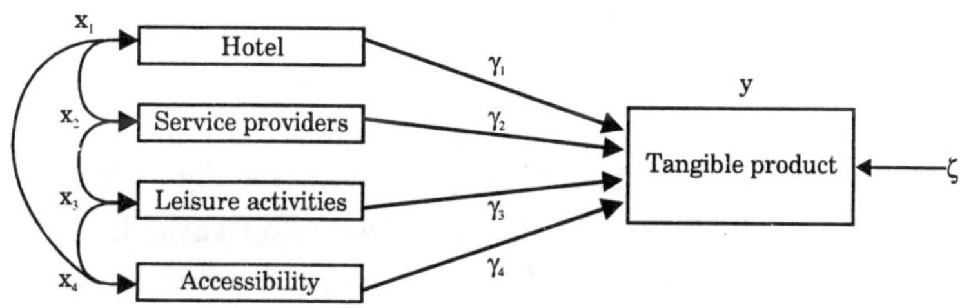

Fig. 7.2 : A single regression model.

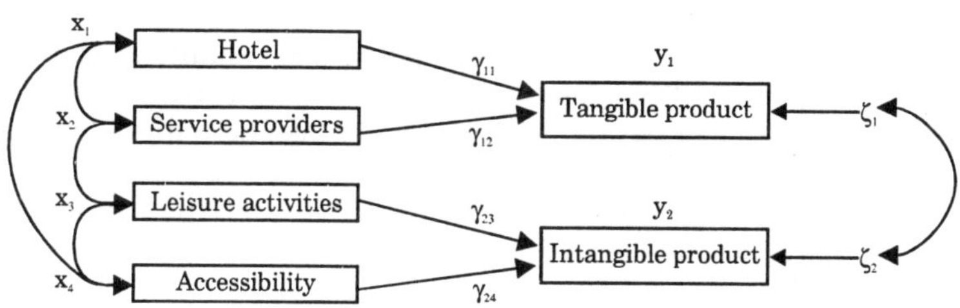

Fig. 7.3 : Bivariate model.

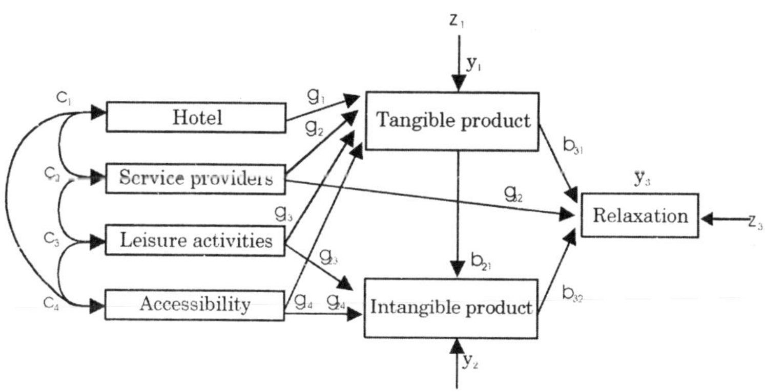

Fig. 7.4 : Recursive model.

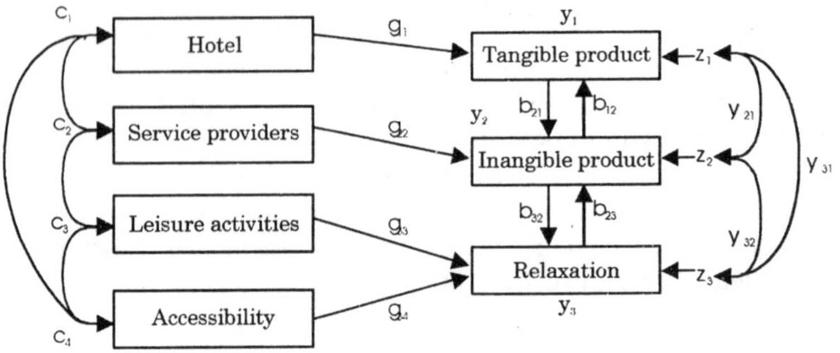

Fig. 7.5 : Non-recursive model.

Full LISREL combines features of Submodel 1 and Submodel 2. It involves x, y, η, ξ, and $\varepsilon, \delta, \zeta$-variables (see Figure 7.6).

Submodel 3 is the LISREL model with no x-variables.

Submodel 3A involves only y, η, ξ and ε, ζ– error variables.

Submodel 3B involves only y and η-variables with no ξ–variables.

The models 3A and 3B are not presented visually as they are parts of the full LISREL model. Since the full LISREL model has a large number of parameters, the advantage of using Submodel 3, rather than the full LISREL is that it has fewer parameter matrices, although each one is large, and it can handle models in which a δ correlates with an ε.

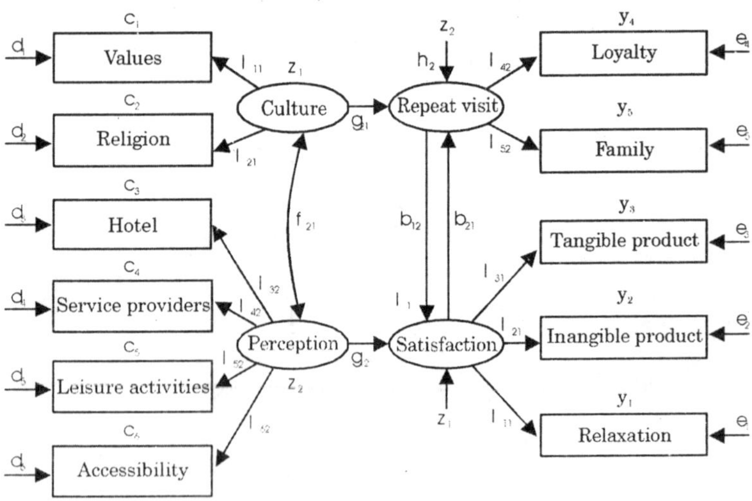

Fig. 7.6 : Full LISREL model.

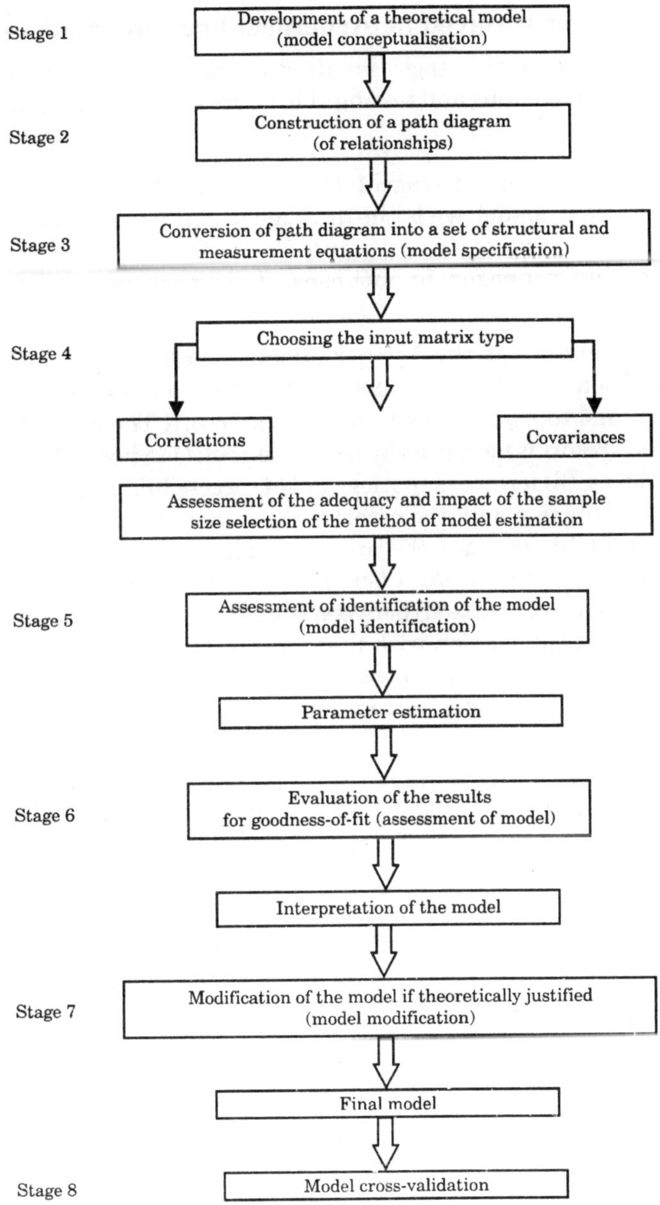

Fig. 7.7 : Stages involved in the application of structural equation modelling.

The Stages Involved in Structural Equation Modelling

There are eight stages involved in the process of structural equation modelling and testing. These are resented in Figure 7.7.

Stage 1

The first part of stage 1 focuses on the development of a theoretical model with the linkages (defined relationships) between latent constructs and their measurable variables, reflecting proposed hypotheses. This part represents the development of a *structural model.*

For example: the hypothesised model consists of two dimensions (latent constructs); tourist perceptions of a beach resort and tourist satisfaction with the resort. The perception of a beach resort is measured by perceptions of: (1) a hotel, (2) service providers, (3) leisure activities, and (4) accessibility to the resort. The satisfaction with the resort is measured by satisfaction with (1) a tangible product, 92) an intangible product (service), and (3) degree of relaxation. It is hypothesised that there is a strong relationship (correlation) between the perception of a beach resort and tourist satisfaction with the resort (Submodel 1) (see Figure 7.1). It can also be hypothesised that tourist satisfaction is determined by tourist perceptions of this resort (full LISREL) (see Figure 7.6).

The second part of stage 1 involves the operationalisation of the latent constructs via the measured variables and describing the way in which they are represented by empirical indicators

Table 7.1
Two-construct Measurement Model

Variables/indicators	*Indicators*	*Loadings on constructs*
	Perception	Satisfaction
Hotel (x_1)	L1	
Service providers (x_2)	L2	
Leisure activities (x_3)	L3	
Accessibility (x_4)	L4	
Tangible product (x_5)		L5
Intangible product (x_6)		L6
Relaxation (x_7)		L7

(manifest variables). This part represents the development of a *measurement model.* The hypothetical measurement model is represented simply by a two-construct model (perception and satisfaction) as shown in Table 7.1.

The first part of stage 1 also provides informaiton about the validities and reliabilities of the vriables. The analysis is predominantly confirmatory because it determines the extent to which the proposed model is consistent with the empirical data.

Critical points

The most critical point at this stage is to include all key predictive variables (multiple indicators of the latent variables) to avoid a specification error. The justification for inclusion of the specific latent constructs and their indicators in a model can be provided by factor analysis. However, this inclusion together must be theoretically sound and be weighted against the limitations of SEM and computer programmes. A model should contain at most twenty variables (five to six constructs each measured by three to four indicators) (Bentler and Chou, 1987). The interpretation of the results of their statistical significance becomes difficult as the number of concepts becomes large (exceeding twenty).

Stage 2

Stage 2 involves the construction of a path diagram. In order to understand the geometric symbols represented in models and correctly draw a path diagram. LISREL requires familiarity with the Greek letters describing LISREL matrices. The Greek letters were presented previously.

In a path diagram all relationships between constructs and their indicators are graphically presented with arrows. They form a visual presentation of the hypotheses and the measurement scheme. A curved line indicates a correlation covariance between constructs, e.g., between perceptions and satisfaction (Submodel 1) (see Figure 7.1). A straight arrow indicates a direct relationship from a construct to its indicators and direct effect relationship between constructs. The direct arrow from perceptions to satisfaction changes the Submodel 1 into a full LISREL analysis (with y-variables) by stating that perception determines satisfaction (see Figure 7.6).

All constructs fall into two categories: exogenous and endogenous. Exogenous constructs are independent variables and are not determined by any other variable in a model (there are no straight arrows pointing to these constructs, e.g. perception in full LISREL). Endogenous constructs are determined by other constructs and relationships contained in the model (there are arrows pointing to these constructs, e.g., satisfaction in full LISREL). They can also determine other endogenous constructs. In order to avoid specification error, attention has to be paid not to omit any exogenous or endogenous constructs.

A path diagram should show all relationships. The number of paths should be theoretically justified. All relationships are to be linear.

Stage 3

Stage 3 involves the formal mathematical specification of the model by describing the nature and number of parameters to be estimated (which variables measure which constructs), translating the path diagram into a series of linear equations that link constructs, and translating the specified model into LISREL language in the form of matrices, indicating hypothesised correlations among constructs or variables. The coefficient matrices represent the paths in a model.

Because both constructs in the hypothetical path diagram are exogenous (Submodel 1), the measurement model and associated correlation matrices for exogenous constructs and indicators are needed. The appropriate LISREL notation is shown in Table 7.2.

At this stage a distinction must be made between fixed, constrained, and free parameters. Fixed parameters specify values a priori and they are not estimated as part of the model. An example of a fixed parameter would be to assign $\lambda_{11} = 1.00$ so that λ_{21}, λ_{31} and λ_{41} would be compared against correlations when all parameters are free. Restricted (constrained) parameters are unknown and are estimated by the model. Example: when two independent variables (ξ_1 and ξ_2) have the same impact on a dependent variable (η_1) one can specify that $\gamma_{11} = \gamma_{12}$ (γ=correlation between latent constructs). In this case it is only necessary to estimate one parameter to determine the value of the other parameter. Free parameters have unknown values, are not constrained to be equal to any other parameter, and need to be estimated by the programme.

Table 7.2
LISREL Notation for the Measurement Model

Exogenous indicator		*Exogenous construct*		*Error*
x_1	=	$\lambda x_{11}\xi_1$	+	δ_1
x_2	=	$\lambda x_{21}\xi_1$	+	δ_2
x_3	=	$\lambda x_{31}\xi_1$	+	δ_3
x_4	=	$\lambda x_{41}\xi_1$	+	δ_4
x_5	=	$\lambda x_{52}\xi_2$	+	δ_5
x_6	=	$\lambda x_{62}\xi_2$	+	δ_6
x_7	=	$\lambda x_{72}\xi_2$	+	δ_7
Correlation among exogenous constructs (ϕ)				
	ξ_1	ξ_2		
ξ_1	–			
ξ_2	ϕ_{21}	–		

λ–correlation between manifest variables and latent constructs ξ.

The LISREL analysis run is based on control commands, which consist of several lines. The LISREL control lines and the input are explained in the LISREL SPSS manuals. Since there are five LISREL submodels different input files need to be requested for each model. The control commands for each submodel should be developed according to the instructions given in the LISREL manual. Also, the correct specification of each line depends on the research phenomena under study. Once the LISREL programme is run it reproduces all command files. The matrix and the parameter specification should be immediately inspected to make sure that no errors have been made.

Stage 4

Stage 4 considers whether the variance/covariance or correlation matrix is to be used as the input data, and this involves an assessment of the sample size. The covariance matrix is used when the objective is to test a theory, provide comparisons between different populations or samples, or to explain the total variance of constructs needed to test the theory. However, because the diagonal of the matrix is not one, interpretation of the results is more difficult because the coefficients must be interpreted in terms of the units of measure for the constructs. The correlation matrix allows for direct comparisons of the coefficients within a model. Therefore, it is more widely used. The correlation matrix is also used to understand the patterns of relationships between the constructs. It is not used to explain the total variance of a construct as needed in theory testing. Thus, interpretation of the results and their generalisability to different situations should be made with caution when the correlation matrix is used. The correlation matrix for the hypothesised model is presented in Table 7.3.

Table 7.3
Correlation Matrix for the Hypothesised Model

Variables	*Hotel* (x_1)	*Service providers* (x_2)	*Leisure activities* (x_3)	*Access* (x_4)	*Tangible product* (x_5)	*Intangible product* (x_6)	*Relaxation* (x_7)
x_1 Hotel	1.000						
x_2 Providers	-0.349	1.000					
x_3 Leisure	0.562	0.786	1.000				
x_4 Access	0.612	0.677	0.432	1.000			
x_5 Tangible	0.899	0.231	0.521	0.421	1.000		
x_6 Intangible	0.123	0.899	0.789	0.513	0.222	1.000	
x_7 Relaxation	0.433	0.335	0.788	0.188	0.111	0.654	1.000

The most widely used method for computing the correlations or covariances between manifest variables is Pearson product-moment correlation and the correlation matrix is computed using Prelis (Joreskog and Sorbom, 1988).

Sample Size

Sample size plays an important role in estimating and interpreting SEM results as well as estimating sampling errors. Although there is no correct rule for estimating sample size for SEM, recommendations are for a size ranging between 100 to 200 (Hair *et al.*, 1995). A sample of 200 is called a 'critical sample size'. The sample size should also be large enough when compared with the number of estimated parameters (as a rule of thumb at least five times the number of parameters), but with an absolute minimum of fifty respondents. The sample size depends on methods of model estimation, which are discussed later.

After the structural and measurement models are specified and the input data type is selected, the computer programme for model estimation should be chosen. There are many various programmes available on the market. Although some offer different advantages, the LISREL computing programme has been the most widely used programme.

Stage 5

Stage 5 addresses the issue of model identification, that is, the extent to which the information provided by the data is sufficient to enable parameter estimation. If a model is not identified, then it is not possible to determine the model parameters. A necessary condition for the identification is that the number of independent parameters is less than or equal to the number of elements of the sample matrix of covariances among the observed variables.

For example: if t parameters are to be estimated, the minimum condition for identification is:

$$t \leq s$$

where $s = 1/2(p+q.)\,(p+q+1)$

p = number of y-variables

q = number of x-variables

- If $t = s$ the set of parameters is *just identified* (there is only one and only one estimate for each parameter).
- If $t<s$, the model is *overidentified* (it is possible to obtain several estimates of the same parameter).
- If $t>s$, the model is *unidentified* (an infinite number of values of the parameters could be obtained).

In a just-identified model, all the information available is used to estimate parameters and there is no information left to test the model (df=0). In an overidentified model there are positive degrees of freedom (equal to $s - t$), thus, one set of estimates can be used to test the model. In the unidentified model, one must either: (1) add more manifest variables; (2) set certain parameters to zero; or (3) set parameters equal to each other (Aaker and Bagozzi, 1979) to make all the parameters identified. However, all three steps can be applied if they are justified by theory.

The condition $t \leq s$ is necessary, but not sufficient, for the identification of a LISREL model. In fact, there are no sufficient conditions for the full structure model. The LISREL programme provides warnings about identification problems.

Identification Problems

The symptoms of potential identification problems are—

(a) very large standard errors for coefficients,

(b) the inability of the programme to invert the information matrix,

(c) impossible estimates (e.g., negative and non-significant error variances for any construct),

(d) high correlations (± 0.80 or above) among observed variables.

These symptoms must be searched out and eliminated.

Sources of Identification Problems

There are several sources of identification problems—

(1) A large number of coefficients relative to the number of correlations or covariances, indicated by a small number of degrees of freedom—similar to the problems of overfitting, that is, insufficient sample size.

(2) The use of reciprocal effects (two-way arrows between the constructs).

(3) Failure to fix the scale of a construct, that is, incorrect assignment of parameters as fixed or free.

(4) Skewness.

(5) Nonlinearity.

(6) Heteroscedasticity.

(7) Multicollinearity.

(8) Singularity.

(9) Autocorrelation.

It should be noted that heteroscedasticity, caused either by non-normality of the variables or the lack of a direct relationship between variables, is not fatal to an analysis. The linear relationship between variables is captured by the analysis but there is even more predictability if the heteroscedasticity is accounted for as well. If it is not, the analysis is wakened, but not invalidated.

Multicollinearity and singularity are problems with a correlation matrix that occur when variables are too highly correlated. For multicollinearity, the variables are very highly correlated (0.8 and above); and for singularity, the variables are perfectly correlated and one of the variables is a combination of one or more of the other variables. When variables are multicollinear or singular, they contain redundant information and they are not all needed in the analysis.

Solutions to Identification Problems

The potential solutions for identification problems are to—

(1) Eliminate some of the estimated coefficients (deleting paths from the path diagram).

(2) Fix the measurement error variances of constructs if possible; if negative change to 0.005.

(3) Fix any structural coefficients that were reliably known, that is, eliminate correlations over one because of multicollinearity of variables.

(4) Remove multicollinearity by using data reduction methods like Principal Components Analysis.

(5) Eliminate troublesome variables, e.g., highly correlated variables, redundant variables.

(6) Check univariate descriptive statistics for accuracy (e.g. out-of-range values, plausible standard deviations, coefficients of variation).

(7) Check for missing values.

(8) Identify non-normal variables, e.g., check for skewness and kurtosis.

(9) Check for outliers.

(10) Check for non-linearity and heteroscedasticity.

(11) Reformulate the theoretical model to provide more constructs relative to the number of relationships examined.

Estimation Methods

The LISREL programme offers different kinds of parameter estimation methods—

- Instrumental Variables (IV).
- Two-stage Least Squares (TSLS).
- Unweighted Least Squares (ULS).
- Generalised Least Squares (GLS).
- Maximum Likelihood (ML).
- Generally Weighted Least Squares (WLS).
- Diagonally Weighted Least Squares (DWLS).

The most widely used are the Two-stage Least Square (TSLS) and Maximum Likelihood Estimation (MLE) methods. The TSLS method computes the initial estimates, and the MLE method computes the final solution. The TSLS method (as well as the IV method) of model estimation is non-iterative and fast. The MLE method (as well as ULS, GLS, WLS and DWLS methods) is an iterative procedure and it successively improves initial parameter estimates. The MLE method may be used to estimate parameters under the assumption of multivariate normality and is robust against departures from normality. When using the MLE method the standard errors (SE) and Chi-square goodness-of-fit measures

Table 7.4
Initial Estimates (TSLS)

Variables	*Perception*	*Satisfaction*
Hotel	0.866	0.000
Service providers	0.847	0.000
Leisure activities	0.801	0.000
Accessibility	0.702	0.000
Tangible product	0.000	0.780
Intangible product (service)	0.000	0.923
Relaxation	0.000	0.930
	Perception	*Satisfaction*
Perception	1.000	
Satisfaction	0.664	1.000

may be used if interpreted with caution. The MLE method is also more precise in large samples. The minimum sample size to ensure appropriate use of MLE is 100. As the sample increases the sensitivity of the method to detect differences among the data also increases. However, as the sample exceeds 400–500 the

Table 7.5
LISREL Estimates (Maximum Likelihood)

Variables	*Perception*	*Satisfaction*
Hotel	0.863	0.000
Service providers	0.849	0.000
Leisure activities	0.805	0.000
Accessibility	0.695	0.000
Tangible product	0.000	0.775
Intangible product (service)	0.000	0.929
Relaxation	0.000	0.931
	Perception	*Satisfaction*
Perception	1.000	
Satisfaction	0.666	1.000

method becomes 'too sensitive' and almost any difference is detected, making all fit measures poor (Hair *et al.*, 1995). The initial and final estimates computed by TSLS and MLE methods for the hypothetical model are presented in Tables 7.4 and 7.5.

A comparison of the TSLS with those of the final ML estimates reveals that they are very accurate. No difference is larger than 0.02.

Types of Solution

The LISREL programme also offers three types of solution:

(1) Non-standardised

(2) Standardised

(3) Completely standardised

Non-standardised Solution

In the non-standardised solution all latent and manifest variables are non-standardised. The non-standardised parameter estimates show the resulting change in a dependent variable from a unit change in an independent variable, all other variables being held constant. Non-standardised coefficients are computed with all variables in their original metric form and describe the effect that variables have in an absolute sense. Thus, they can be used to compare similar models in other populations. However, they are tied to the measurement units of the variables they represent. Any change in the measurement unit for an independent or dependent variable changes the value and comparability of parameters across populations (Bagozzi, 1977).

Standardised Solution

In the standardised solution only latent variables (constructs) are standardised and the manifest variables (x and y) are left in their original metric.

Completely Standardised Solution

In the completely standardised solution both the latent and the manifest variables are standardised. The standardised parameters reflect the resulting change in a dependent variable from a standard deviation change in an independent variable. The standardised parameters are appropriate to compare the relative contributions of a number of independent variables on the same dependent variable and for the same sample of observations. They are not appropriate to compare across populations or samples (Bagozzi, 1980).

Stage 6

Stage 6 involves the assessment of the model fit using a variety of fit measures for the measurement and structural model (and supporting/rejecting the proposed hypotheses). However, before evaluating the goodness-of-fit between the data and model several assumptions of SEM must be met.

SEM Assumptions

Assumptions of SEM are—

(1) Independence of variables.

(2) Random sampling of respondents.

(3) Linearity of all relationships between variables, latent and observed.

(4) Multivariate normality of distribution (important in the use of LISREL).

(5) No kurtosis and no skewness.

(6) Appropriate data measured on interval or ratio scale.

(7) Sample size 100–400.

(8) Exploratory purpose of the study.

The above assumptions can be tested through programme LISREL. The Generalised Least Squares (GLS), which is an alternative estimation method, can adjust for the violations of these assumptions. However, as the models become large and complex, the use of this method becomes more limited.

Additionally, if the use of SEM is associated with time-series data, considerable care is required to test for autocorrelation and stationarity, and where required the data transformed into a non-stationary series.

Offending Estimates

Once the assumptions are met, the results must first be examined for offending estimates, which are coefficients that exceed acceptable limits. The common examples are—

- negative error variances or non-significant error variances for any construct,
- standardised coefficients exceeding or every close to 1.0,
- very large standard errors associated with any estimated coefficient.

These offending estimates must be resolved before evaluating the model results. In the case of negative error variances (Heywood case) the offending error variances can be changed to a very small positive value (0.005). If correlations in the standardised solution exceed 1.0, or two estimates are highly correlated, one of the constructs should be removed. Tables 7.6 and 7.7 present the Heywood case.

Tables 7.6 and 7.7 show that a loading for tangible product is greater than 1.0 (known as a Heywood case). A corresponding negative error measurement value for the same variable is derived (–0.325). Such estimates are inappropriate and must be corrected before the model can be interpreted and the goodness-of-fit assessed. In this case, the variable will be retained and the corresponding negative error variance will be set to a small value of 0.005 to ensure that the loading will be less than 1.0. The model is then re-estimated. Since in examining the new results, no offending estimates are found (a new loading on a tangible product is 0.996 and error variance is 0.005). The model can be assessed for its goodness-of-fit.

Table 7.6
Initial Results of the Measurement Model

Variables	*Perception*	*Satisfaction*
Hotel	0.644	0.000
Service providers	0.743	0.000
Leisure activities	0.564	0.000
Accessibility	0.432	0.000
Tangible product	0.000	**1.234**
Intangible product (service)	0.000	0.685
Relaxation	0.000	0.879

Table 7.7
Measurement Error for Indicators

Variables	*Hotel*	*Service providers*	*Leisure activities*	*Accessibility*	*Tangible product*	*Intangible product*	*Relaxation*
Hotel	0.585						
Service Providers	0.000	0.572					
Leisure activities	0.000	0.000	0.453				
Accessibility	0.000	0.000	0.000	0.321			
Tangible product	0.000	0.000	0.000	0.00	**-0.325**		
Intangible product	0.000	0.000	0.000	0.000	0.000	1.422	
Relaxation	0.000	0.000	0.000	0000	0.000	0.000	0.000

When assessing model fit, attention must be paid both to the measurement and the structural models. Fornell (1987) suggested simultaneous evaluation of both models. However, Anderson and Gerbing (1982) reported that proper evaluation of the measurement model (latent variables) is a pre-requisite of the evaluation of the structural model (the analysis of the relations among the latent variables). The LISREL programme runs the assessment of both models simultaneously.

Types of Fit Measurement

There are three types of fit measurement—

- *Absolute fit measures* (assess the overall model fit, both structural and measurement together, with no adjustment for overfitting).
- *Incremental fit measures* (compare the proposed model to a comparison model).
- *Parsimonious fit measures* (adjust the measures of fit to compare models with different numbers of coefficients and determine the fit achieved by each coefficient). In order to achieve a better understanding of the acceptability of the proposed model multiple measures should be applied.

Absolute Fit Measures

The absolute fit measures provide information on the extent to which the model *as a whole* provides an acceptable fit to the data. They are evaluated by—

- Likelihood ratio of Chi-square to the degrees of freedom (the acceptable range is between 0.05 and 0.10-0.20). A large value of Chi-square indicates a poor fit of the model to the data; a small value of Chi-square indicates a good fit. The degrees of freedom judge whether the Chi-square is large on small. The number of degrees of freedom is calculated as—

$$df = 1/2[(p + q)(p + q + 1)] - t$$

where p = the number of endogenous indicators

q = the number of exogenous indicators

$p + q$ = number of manifest variables

t = the number of independent parameters to be estimated.

- Goodness-of-fit index (GFI), which is an indicator of the relative amount of variances and covariances jointly accounted for by the model, shows how closely the proposed model comes to a perfect one (takes values between 0 and 1 and the closer to unity, the better the model fit). A marginal acceptance level is 0.90.
- Root mean square residuals (RMSR) reflect the average amount of variances and covariances not accounted for by the model. The closer to zero, the better the fit. A marginal acceptance level is 0.80. RMSR must be interpreted in

relation to the sizes of the observed variances and covariances.

- Root mean square error of approximation (RMSEA).
- Non-centrality parameter (NCP).
- Scaled non-centrality parameter (SNCP).
- Expected cross-validation index (ECVI).

The NCP, SNCP and ECVI are used in comparison among alternative models.

Results in the hypothetical model—

Revised model	
Chi-square	15.87
Degrees of freedom	10
Significance level	0.08
Goodness-of-fit index (GFI)	0.949
Adjusted Goodness-of-fit index (AGFI)	0.889
Root mean square residual (RMSR)	0.056

The Chi-square value (15.87 with 10 df) has a statistical significance level of 0.08, above the minimum level of 0.05, but not above the more conservative levels of 0.10 or 0.20. This statistic shows some support for a notion that the differences between the predicted and actual matrices are non-significant and it indicates an acceptable model fit. The GFI of 0.949 is quite high, but not when adjusted for model parsimony (different number of coefficients). The RMSR indicates that the average residual correlation is 0.056, acceptable given strong correlations in the original correlation matrix.

Problems with Chi-square Statistics

Since these statistics provide overall measures of fit they do not express the quality of the model. It has been argued that the Chi-square measure-of-fit should not be regarded as the best indicator of the model fit, particularly when there is data departure from normality. Lack of normality can inflate the Chi-square statistics and create upward bias for determining significance of the coefficients. Also, the use of Chi-square is not valid in most applications (Joreskog and Sorbom, 1989a).

Although the Chi-square measure may be trated as a test of the hypothesis, the statistical problem is not one of testing a hypothesis (which a priori might be considered false), but one of fitting the model to the data, and deciding whether the fit is adequate or not. Joreskog and Sorbom (1989b) explain that in most empirical work, models are only experimental and regarded as only an approximation to reality, and for this reason the Chi-square should not be used. Other reason for not using a Chi-square as criteria for judging the adequacy of the model include sample size and problems related to the power of the test. Large samples tend to increase the Chi-square due to specification error in the model. Thus, Chi-square statistics should be interpreted with caution.

GFI, AGFI and RMSR Measures

Measures such as GFI, AGFI and RMSR also do not express perfectly the quality of the models. According to Joreskog and Sorbom (1989b), quality should be judged by other internal and external criteria such as theoretical grounding. For instance, these measures can show poor fit because of one relationship only being poorly determined. Thus, a fit of 0.5-0.6 does not precisely state whether the model *is* or *is not* supported by the data. In practice, it can suggest that some of the poorly described relationship paths should be eliminated from the model to make it more sound, and the model should be run again to see if an improved fit could be obtained. These measures also do not indicate what is wrong with the model (Joreskog and Sorbom, 1989b). As to the RMSR, they work best of *all* observed variables are standardised.

The Incremental Fit Measures

While all the absolute measures might fall within acceptable levels, the incremental fit and parsimonious fit indices are needed to ensure acceptability of the model from other perspectives. The incremental fit measures assess the incremental fit of the model compared to a null model (the most simple model that can be theoretically justified, e.g., a single construct model related to all indicators with no measurement error). These are—

(1) Tucker-Lewis measure (TL);

(2) Normed fit index (NFI).

These incremental fit measures should exceed the recommended level of minimum 0.90 to support acceptance of the proposed model.

Results in the hypothetical model—

Null Model	
Chi-square	210.876
Degrees of freedom	15
Significance level	0.000
Tucker Lewis (TL)	0.9414

Both incremental fit measures exceed the recommended level of 0.90 and support acceptance of the proposed model.

Parsimonious Fit Measures

Parsimonious fit measures determine the model fit in comparison to models of differing complexity. The fit is compared versus the number of estimated coefficients (or degrees of freedom) needed to achieve the level of fit (fit per coefficient). The two most appropriate parsimonious fit measures are—

- Normed Chi-square (Chi-square/df) (the level recommended by Carmines and Mclver (1981) is between 1.0 and 3.0).
- Adjusted for the degrees of freedom goodness-of-fit index (AGFI) (takes values between 0 and 1; and the closer to unity, the better the model fit). If there is a drop in AGFI as compared to GFI, the overall fit of the model can be questioned.

Results in the hypothetical model show that the normed Chi-square (Chi-square divided by degrees of freedom) is 1587 (15.87/10). This falls within the recommended levels of 1.0 to 3.0. The AGFI value of 0.889 is close to the recommended level of 0.90. These results show support for model parsimony.

In summary, the various measures of overall model goodness-of-fit gave support to the results of an acceptable representation of the hypothesised constructs.

The other parsimonious fit measures are—

- Parsimony normed fit index (PNFI).
- Parsimonious goodness-of-fit index (PGFI).

- Comparative fit index (CFI).
- Incremental fit index (IFI).
- Relative fit index (RFI).
- Critical N (CN).

Squared Multiple Correlation Coefficients

The fit of the *measurement model* is assessed by examining squared multiple correlation coefficients (SMC) for the *y*- and *x*-variables, which indicate how well the *y*- and *x*-variables measure the latent construct, the largest amount of variance accounted for by the constructs, and the extent to which the individual variables are free from measurement error. They also represent the reliabilities (convergent validities) of these measures. These coefficients lie between 0 and 1 (the closer to 1, the better the variable acts as an indicator of the latent construct).

Results in the hypothetical model—

Squared multiple correlations for x-variables

Hotel	Providers	Leisure	Access	Tangible	Intangible	Relaxation
0.745	0.720	0.648	0.483	0.600	0.863	0.867

The results show that all *x*-variables are good measurements of both constructs.

The total coefficients of determination (TCD) (R^2) for all *y*- and *x*-variables provide measures of how well the *y*-and *x*-variables *as a group* measure the latent constructs. The closer to 1, the better. Results in the hypothetical model show that total, coefficient of determination for *x*-variables is 0.981. All *x*-variables as a group measure the latent constructs very well.

The fit of the *structural model* is assessed by the squared multiple correlations (SMC) for structural equations, which indicates the amount of variance in each endogenous latent variable accounted for by the independent variables in the relevant structural equation, and the total coefficient of determination (TCD) (R^2) for structural equations, which shows the strength of the relationships for all structural relationships together. Results in the hypothetical model show that the R^2 for the total structural equations is 0.788.

Multi-collinearity

The results of structural equation modelling can be affected by multicollinearity as in regression. If large values of correlation for the observed variables appear the deletion of one variable, or reformulation of the relationships should be considered. Although there is no limit on what defines high correlation, values exceeding 0.90 and even 0.80 can indicate problems, values below 0.8 can be compensated for by declaring covariance paths between independent variable. That is, it is possible to model multicollinearity within the SEM analysis.

Each of the constructs can also be evaluated separately by examining:

- I–values.
- Correlations between the latent constructs.
- Standard errors (SE).
- Fitted residuals (FR).

T-values

The examination of the *t*-values is associated with examining in indicators' loadings (*t*-values for the paths) for statistical significance. If the *t*–values associated with each of the loadings for

Table 7.8
Construct Loadings (*t*–values in parentheses)

Variables	*Perception*	*Satisfaction*
Hotel	0.644 (6.543)	0.000
Service providers	0.788 (7.899)	0.000
Leisure activities	0.655 (8.999)	0.000
Accessibility	0.566 (6.888)	0.000
Tangible product	0.000	0.877 (12.435)
Intangible product (service)	0.000	0.899 (11.456)
Relaxation	0.000	0.901 (12.345)

the path coefficients are larger than 2, the parameters are significant and variables are significantly related to their specified constructs, thus verifying the relationships among indicators and constructs.

The examination of the *t*–values associated with each of the loading in the hypothetical model indicates that for each variable they exceed the critical values for the 0.05 significance level (critical value = 1.96) and the 0.01 significance level as well (critical value = 2.576). Thus, all variables are significantly related to their specified constructs, verifying posited relationships among indicators and constructs (see Table 7.8).

Correlation between the Latent Constructs

The examination of the correlation between the latent constructs is associated with examining the ø values and *t*-values.

Example: correlation among latent constructs (*t*-value in parentheses)

	Perception	*Satisfaction*
Perception	1.000	
Satisfaction	0.899 (14.567)	1.000

The examination of the correlation between the latent constructs and the *t*-value show that the correlation is very high and the *t*-value exceeds the critical value of 1.96, indicating that the latent constructs are significantly correlated with each other.

Standard Errors

The examination of standard errors is associated with assessing the standard errors (SE) for each coefficient and construct. Standard errors show how accurately the values of the parameters are estimated. The smaller the standard errors, the better the estimation. However, what is small or large depends on the units of measurement in latent constructs and the magnitude of the parameter estimate itself. The standard errors are correct under assumptions of multivariate normality. They should be interpreted with caution if the condition of normality does not hold. Therefore, *t*-values are better to be used as independent units of measurement.

Fitted Residuals

The model fit can also be examined by assessing the fitted

residuals (FR), which represent the differences between the observed and the fitted correlations calculated from the model. They should be relatively small to the size of the elements of the correlation matrices to indicate that the fit of the models is acceptable. However, since the fitted residuals depend on the metric of the observed variables (the unit of measurement), they can vary from variable to variable, and are difficult to use in the assessment of fit. The problem is avoided by evaluating the standardized residuals (SR) (fitted residuals divided by their standard errors), which are independent of the metric of the observed variables and can be interpreted as standard normal deviations. An SR that exceeds the value of 2.58 in absolute terms indicates substantial specification and prediction error for a pair of indicators.

Q–plot

The best picture of fit is obtained by looking at the Q-plot, which plots the standardized residuals (horizontal axis) against the quartiles of the normal distribution (vertical axis). The best possible fit is obtained when all residuals lie in a straight vertical line; the worst is when the residuals lie in a horizontal straight line. An acceptable fit is indicated when the residuals lie approximately along the diagonal, with steeper plots (greater than 45°) representing better fits (see Fig. 7.8). If the pattern of residuals is non-linear this indicates departure from normality, linearity and/or specification errors in the model.

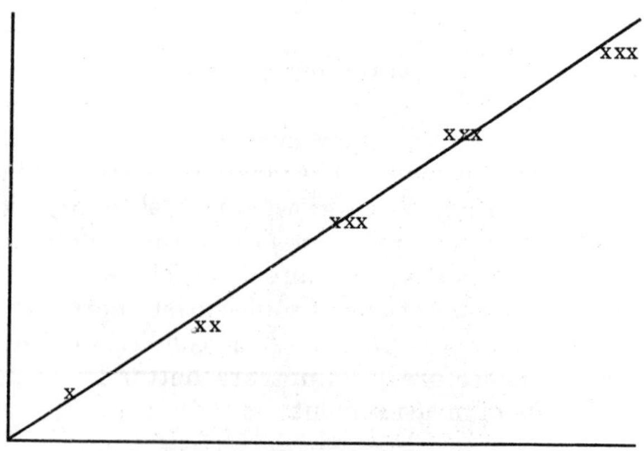

Fig. 7.8 : The Q-plot for the hypothetical model. A model fit is acceptable as the residuals lie along the diagonal.

Stage 7

Stage 7 considers whether modifications to the model have to be made in the light of the results obtained at the previous stage. At this stage the analysis becomes exploratory in nature and results from previous analysis are used to develop a better fitting model. The aim is to identify specification errors and produce a new model that fits the data better. This new model has to be verified on a second independent sample.

Examination of the Standardized Residuals

The first modification to the model may be done through examination of the standardized residuals and the modifications indices. The standardized residuals (normalized) are provided by the programme and represent the differences between the observed correlation/covariance and the estimated correlation/covariance matrix. Residuals values greater than ±2.58 are considered statistically significant at 0.05 level. Significant residuals indicate substantial error for a pair of indicators. The acceptable range is one in twenty residuals exceeding 2.58 by chance. In the hypothetical model only one value exceeded 2.58. Thus, only one correlation from the original input matrix has a statistically significant residual. This falls within the acceptable range.

Deleting or Adding Parameters

The other two ways in which modification to a model can be made is by deleting or adding parameters. In both cases, deleting or adding parameters should be guided by theory. Non-significant t-values can give insight as to which parameters should be eliminated. However, if a theory suggests that particular parameters should be included in the model, even non-significant parameters should be retained because the sample size may be too small to detect their real significance (Joreskog and Sorbom, 1989b).

The effect of the deletion on the model fit can be assessed by comparing the Chi-square values of the two models, particularly the differences in Chi-squares.

When to Use Modification Indices

The modification indices (MI) can be used to decide which parameters should be added to the model. The MI are measures of the predicted decrease in the Chi-square that results if a single parameter (fixed or constrained) is freed (relaxed) and the model re-estimated, with all other parameters maintaining their present values. The improvement in fit from relaxing the parameters is acceptable under the condition that only one parameter is relaxed at a time. The model modification should never be based solely on the MI. Modification of the models must be theoretically justified. Consideration should be given to whether some of the parameters are not necessary to measure the latent constructs. According to Darden (1983), achieving a good fit at all costs is not always recommended because a good fit for a model may theoretically be inappropriate. There are many models that could fit the data better. In fact, a poor fit tells more, that is, the degree to which the model is not supported by the data.

Comparison of Nested Models

If the best fitting model cannot be found using the confirmatory strategy (where the researcher specifies a single model and SEM to assess its significance), then the best fitting model can also be determined by comparison of competing or nested models. Firstly, a number of alternative models are compared to find a model which comes closest to a theory. Differences between models are indicated by the differences in the Chi-square values for the different models. These differences can be tested for statistical significance with the appropriate degrees of freedom. The objective is to find the best fit from among the set of models. Secondly, an initial model goes through a series of model respecifications in order to improve the model fit.

Stage 8

Stage 8 involves the cross-validation of the model with a new data set. This is done by dividing the sample into two parts to conduct a validation test. The LISREL multisample analysis can be used for this purpose. The cross-validation test is performed when modification indices are used and the model did not provide an acceptable fit. This test should also be performed when the model shows an acceptable fit in the first analysis. In addition, cross-validation can be used to compare competing models in terms of predictive validity and facilitate the selection of a model; to compare the difference between samples belonging to different populations and assess the impact of moderating variables (Sharma *et al.*, 1981).

However, cross-validation has, its limitations: (1) it requires access to the raw data and a new data set: (2) the sample must be large enough to divide it into sub-samples and generate reliable estimates (minimum sample size should be between 300–500 observations ; and (3) bias may occur if sample splitting is done randomly.

CONCLUSION

SEM Modelling is a powerful tool enabling researchers to go beyond factor analysis into the arena of determining whether one set of unobserved constructs (dimensions) can determine (be seen to be likely to determine) another set of dimensions. In tourism studies, it is often the case that the variables under study cannot be directly observed or measured (for example, motivation, satisfaction, importance, perception) yet these unobserved variables might be hypothesized to determine one another. SEM analysis is a methodology capable of handling this type of analysis, along with more conventional regression models, and simultaneous regression models, while accounting for multicollinearity and, with appropriate care, other assumptions of regression modelling.

8

Conclusion

This book has attempted to project a balanced approach to the foundations, concepts and issues of ecotourism as they currently exist. At the outset, it was mentioned that there are grounds for maintaining either a positive or negative outlook on where ecotourism has been and where it is going. Perhaps this is the place for more of a personal, introspective look at the phenomenon.

There can be no question that disparate views exist on how and at what level ecotourism ought to be conceptualised and delivered. Like so many other things, it depends on the angle from which one approaches the subject (e.g. economics, marketing, ecology). Admittedly, the approach taken in this book is one that is more protectionist, which has ultimately led to a relatively elaborate definition of ecotourism. Such a view is based on the belief that if ecotourism is to survive it will have to do so by reverting back to or adopting a 'greener' agenda. While some argue, as I do, for a stricter definition of ecotourism, some of my colleagues go so far as to suggest that ecotourism cannot survive without a relationship with sustainable mass tourism. We will have to see. If ecotourism does partner mass tourism, has it not undergone a significant transformation? Is it not then mass sustainable tourism with a sprinkling of nature? I was told as a graduate student that if ecotourism were to become successful, it would have undermined everything that it had initially set out to accomplish.

To me this is fast becoming reality. Those, however, who see ecotourism as the way of the future for all tourism must take need of the words of Wall (1994:9), who wrote that :

> The most important environmental challenge facing tourist planners and managers is not to find a means of inserting small numbers of environmentally aware visitors into pristine environments (although this is certainly a worthy objective); rather it is to devise sustainable forms of mass tourism.

This quotation emphasises the fact that sustainable tourism must lead the way in the future development and management of the tourism industry. Ecotourism is but one type of sustainable tourism (in principle), against a backdrop of many, many other forms. Wall further asks the question, which has been addressed earlier in the book, of whether forms of mass tourism can be developed which are environmentally benign. The research and the many case studies around the world illustrate that mass tourism will have to become more sustainable, especially in light of the growing magnitude of the industry—is there any end in sight? If ecotourism has a role to play in mass tourism's transformation it will be by demonstrating, at a micro scale, the ability of the industry to become more ecologically accountable and responsible through the development of alternative energy strategies, sensitivity to the resource base and local people, and so on. A majority role in this capacity to change, however, will be played by chose involved in sustainable tourism, e.g. Europe, where some of the best research and development in the industry is occurring. We cannot afford to lose sight of how the communities of Europe have initiated many superior programmes and policies that advocate doing more with less.

The issue of mass tourism as ecotourism pertains to a related problem surrounding ecolabelling and resort development. Personally, I worry when I see names like Ramada on ecolodge signs, which is the case in a recently developed ecoresort in the Yucatan Peninsula of Mexico. This concern is not necessarily from the perspective of ecological impact (Ramada has apparently adopted an environmental integrity image in its product development, as have other hotel giants such as Holiday Inn), but rather from a socio-economic perspective. One of the tenets of ecotourism was that it is suppose to be locally oriented. How will Ramada remain internationally competitive if it is pouring its revenues into the local Sirons community and the preservation of biodiversity of the region? Flares are automatically discharged when the international business community gets involved in such 'local' enterprises. This scenario is more along the lines of what Britton (1977) and others suggest about metropolitan domination of the industry. In my estimation, one of the biggest threats facing the ecotourism industry today, as implied earlier is the danger that the large hotel and resort corporations will infiltrate the ecotourism industry with less than altruistic ends. Let the large mega-resorts and mass tourism become sustainable tourism, not ecotourism.

Canadian Pacific Hotels and Resorts, for example, has recently developed more environmentally friendly policies as a result of a formal survey of its thousands of employees (D'Amore 1993). Its 12-point environmental action plan is indeed a laudable example of leadership in this area. Would such policies have appeared popular 15 years ago? Not likely. Ramada and other hotel chains are responding to what they perceive as a movement in public opinion on the management of hotels. There appears to be a good deal of business savvy in this choice (i.e., they benefit the hotel in terms of lower maintenance and overhead costs, but also the customer in the sense of peace of mind), but is that all it is? It reminds me of the recent trend for big companies to provide health memberships for their workers on the assumption that there is a genuine interest in the health and well-being of employees. The underlying principle of this provision may be that employees are encouraged to get fit and in the process be more productive on the job with less absenteeism, and with the ultimate end of saving the corporation money. In cases such as this where there seems to be a win-win situation, it is hard to argue against the fact that the corporation is doing nothing more than treating the worker as a commodity with the ultimate goal of extracting the maximum yield out of this resource. I do not wish to be too pessimistic, but it is difficult to determine whether the motives of the hotels are truly intrinsic (principled actions) or extrinsic (economic gain) in nature. One wonders about the lengths to which hotels and other businesses would go to remain successful if resource protection and environmental concerns were not contingent upon financial success and public opinion.

A key issue to address in the future is the role that government and industry play in the delivery of the ecotourism product. There is no question that the private sector, when left to its own designs, will strive to make money. Given this axiom, if ecotourism fails, should the responsibility for its demise lie squarely on the shoulders of the operators? Not directly. More appropriately, I believe, fault should lie in the hands of national governments and international organisations involved in directing tourism development, for their inability to provide leadership and implement appropriate guidelines or regulations within the industry. In addition, government-sponsored research must be completed responsibly. In some cases marketers and consultants have seen fit to rationalise ecotourism's market potential and therefore overall economic impact through irresponsible methodological approaches, which has, in part, contributed to the erosion of the concept. We have allowed marketing to dictate experiences rather than *vice versa*.

Some of the critics of ecotourism argue that (1) it must operate at low levels or carrying capacities on order for it to become successful, and as a result (2) it may not be sufficient to allow all members of a community to benefit economically. Communities are defined as such by the diversity of human and physical resources that they comprise. Just as in ecosystems, members of the community have roles to play and niches to occupy. The same principle holds true in an economics context. Development theory posits that economic viability is very much a function of a balanced approach to economic development. Just as monocultures are a threat in an ecological context, regions bent on establishing ecotourism as the only form of economic development are subject to the same dysfunctions. Such regions should be well aware of the fact that ecotourism must be integrated into a broader sustainable development policy, which constitutes strong planning and management of the resource and the industry. Both planning and management are critical to the delivery of ecotourism, and must occur through the institutional arrangements that have been put in place to allow for it to occur, i.e. rules, laws, regulations, and so on—which is leadership that must come from government. A poorly run industry does not a poorly conceived idea make.

Critics of ecotourism further charge that the definitions and goals of ecotourism are far too lofty, i.e. there is very little chance that all aspects of elaborate definitions can be reached. This argument is a valid one that nevertheless should be examined. Essentially there are two ways of dealing with it : (1) to agree, and modify the definition to be more forgiving, which is the prevailing norm; or (2) to argue that we must set lofty goals in order to accomplish prescribed ends. In support of the latter, the rationale is that the establishing of certain objectives, or principles of ecotourism, induces practitioners and researchers to be true to these ends. In addition, it enables, in much the same way as the design of the accreditation programme in Australia, the attainment of a means by which to separate operators on the basis of established criteria. Elitist? Not really; it provides the consumer with needed information in making informed decisions on product content.

Oscar Wilde said that a critic is 'a man who knows the price of everything, and the value of nothing'. In my estimation, the real job that lies ahead is not in writing off ecotourism (this is too easy), but rather in striving to build clarity and meaning into the concept through some fundamental restricting. Perhaps we just need to play better by the rules, but in the case of ecotourism the rules have yet to be fully agreed upon. Sustainable development has its critics, but at the same time there are few other options to look to for a greener future. Will there be any new substitutes for ecotourism to look to on the horizon (e.g. 'deep ecotourism')? Most likely not. Ecotourism was suppose to be tourism's Deep Ecology. As yet, according to many case studies around the world, it is not, and it will not be until we address some fundamental issues related to its philosophy and delivery. The vision for the future of ecotourism (and sustainable tourism) is not universally shared either from the perspective of the industry (tourists, local people, and the industry) or geographically–as a collective calling or dream. We must view the environment and its relationship to tourism as being like a bank: we keep withdrawing without making any deposits, and while such deposits could be earning valuable interest in the form of a stronger human-land relationship and a better way to conduct commerce, the withdrawals we make serve to intensify the dichotomy that exists between people and the natural world. To this end I have heard ecotourism referred to as being rather like a game of pick-up sticks. One must carefully isolate a stick from a pile of sticks and remove it without disturbing the others. The analogy to be made is that when tourists venture off into wilderness settings they must be wary of disturbing the other members of the community (plants and animals) with which they are interacting. However, pick-up sticks is about removing as many of the sticks as possible without disturbing the others, until there are no sticks left. In ecotourism, indeed in all forms of land use, we must learn to recognise when enough is enough.

Towards the end of 1997 I had the opportunity to sit in on the deliberations of a provincial meeting not the development of the ecotourism product along the Trans-Canada Highway. The feeling was that rather than travel through a province, and hence view the highway simply as a medium of transportation, tourists should instead be encouraged to stop to enjoy some of the wonderful Ecotourism sites along the way. This association of interested people grew as a consequence of the Trans-Canada Highway ecotours developed by Environment Canada in the 1970s and 1980s to allow people travelling on the highway (see Chapter 2) to enjoy natural attractions of various regions across Canada. However, whereas the Environment Canada publications were not developed with a profit motive in mind–they were simply a programme designed to strengthen the human-land relationship in Canadians and international travellers–the more recent meetings on the Trans-Canada Highway took on a very different form. There was an overriding emphasis on measuring success only in terms of the economic return from efforts put into marketing the product. There is no question that as the world's largest industry, tourism is very much about the profit motive, and, as outlined earlier, ecotourism happens to be the fastest-growing segment of the industry. In this meeting, however, there were decidedly few who could not see the tourist as more than a monetary symbol. It made me wonder whether anything would be gained or accomplished if a person, visiting any given eco-attraction along the stretch of highway, did not spend a dime at a Trans-Canada ecotour site. So, what determines success of ecotourism ventures? People making money, or tourists gaining rewarding experiences, or, indeed, both? Does the market really reflect the numbers of ecotourists reported these days, or is it simply the industry manufacturing and repackaging the product into ecotourism-like experiences for a public that is less than devoted to this form of travel? The reader will not find the answer to this question here, but nevertheless it is a question that needs to be addressed. Ecotourism is far too 'sexy' these days to be ignored by an industry bent on profit.

I thought again of ecolabelling when the chair of the meeting suggested that we 'take a broader look at ecotourism', including any cultural and natural attractions. What other types of attractions are there? Isn't it the same as the example of helicopter ecotourism in Hollywood. But what about the differences between our helicopter in Hollywood and our hard core ecotourist flying to Costa Rica? Which is more intrusive? There are those who argue that the former would in fact be less ecologically disruptive than having people traipsing through sensitive rainforests; after all, those in the helicopter aren't touching the ground. But yet the helicopter seems fundamentally wrong, for one reason or another. The answer could be that in order for the experience to occur, the ecotourist must have some tangible, concrete connection to the natural world. This means seeing it, feeling it, touching it–sensing it. All involve a type of learning that cannot occur in the helicopter; hence there is not the opportunity of getting 'into' nature. Also, is it the helicopter itself that is the main attraction, or the content of the experience (i.e. the interpretation of Hollywood)? Finally, how does it contribute to conservation? Would it be any more acceptable to take a helicopter flight over the Swiss Alps or over the Blue Mountains of Australia? Perhaps. But if helicopter flights over Hollywood become ecotourism, then anything can become ecotourism. The vultures are circling.

I have often contemplated the relationship that exists between tourism and recreation. Pleasure tourism falls within the realm of leisure and recreation. It is, therefore, a form of recreation and, like many of these forms, it involves spending money. However, recreation is also much more. It often brings out the best in community development and advocates accessibility in allowing others who are less fortunate to participate. Tourism, on the other hand, is elitist–not everyone can afford to travel–and is one of the best examples of the division between the haves and have-nots. The spirit of the provision of recreation services in the public and not-for-profit sectors has much more influence in the planning and programming of events than it does in tourism. There is the sense in tourism that events (tours) can be planned only with the profit motive in hand. However, will there ever be a day when tourism exists as more than just a vehicle for the private sector to make money, at the expense of accessibility? In recreation the experience occurs through the development of programmes (at least those that are not in the field of marketing); in tourism, we call the programme a product. The two have fundamentally different connotations. While in the future we could look for answers to this dilemma in the not-for-profit sector–which is more likely to have the interests of nature more firmly entrenched in its camp-many such agencies also adhere to a strong profit philosophy.

Like the tourism industry in general, the fate of ecotourism will be controlled, to a certain degree, by unfettered demand. The question which is most pressing, though, is to what extent the international community is willing to let this happen. In simpler terms, will we let ecotourists and the providers of ecotourism services determine the fate of the industry, or rather will the industry require the intervention of other local, region, national, and international bodies to establish direction? There appears to be growing support for the latter, i.e. that regulation within the sustainable tourism and Ecotourism industry is the way of the future. While in many cases this is unpalatable to those working in the industry, again we must look beyond satisfying strictly individual and economic needs to an approach that is sensitive to the needs of the resource base and local people first.

The following list provides some direction in attaining more of the socio-ecological ends of a principled ecotourism culture:

(1) Minimise the number of operators and tourists within ecotour regions in line with the capacity of the environment to absorb the impacts of ecotourism. This implies that significantly more research needs to be done to understand the relationship that exists between tourists, local people, the industry, government, and the resource base.

(2) Conduct further research on the business philosophies of ecotour operators in understanding how they adhere to regional land use strategies. Allow only operators with proven track records to conduct tours. This entails a significant degree of monitoring to evaluate those that comply and those that do not.

(3) Insist that operators maintain a specified level of competence, through accreditation. Insist also that evaluations be conducted by ecotourists and that these

are subject to review by regional review committees (e.g. evaluations to be mailed not to the operator but rather to the committee).

(4) Insist that governments and industry work together to institute fair and equitable guidelines to regulate and/or guide the ecotourism industry.

(5) Research supports the notion that the development of an ecotourism industry should not be imposed on a community, but rather should start from the ground up. Such an approach emphasises the importance of decision-making from within rather than from without. External influences (experts) should be encouraged, but not at the expense of the community's integrity.

(6) Insist that international agencies be encouraged to coordinate research and to provide needed strength in calling attention to situations where the industry will potentially have or has had a significantly negative impact on the resources and people of a region.

(7) Establish stronger linkages between educational institutions and local people by providing such people with the tools (e.g. diplomas, degrees) to work in the industry. These programmes need to be developed in association with the needs of local people, not necessarily the needs of the institutions.

(8) Work to provide a definition of ecotourism and ecotourists which is acceptable to the international community. At present there is little consensus among practitioners and researchers, which is hampering the progress of research in the field.

(9) Develop a template to determine the percentage of ecotourism revenues that should go to local populations, and into the resource base of the host region.

(10) Place more emphasis on addressing the critical absence of focus in ecotourism research, including research theory and methodologies. Included here would be the need to collect data that demonstrate to government and other decision-makers the benefits of ecotourism, especially in

the face of other, more disruptive forms of land use.

(11) Examine international models where trusts have been established from tourism or other types of developments. The purpose of such trusts would be to accumulate money from tourism or other land uses, over time, so that in the event of the demise of the development or industry, the region would be able to maintain financial viability through investment in other industries. A case in point is Shetland, Scotland, which was able to build up a substantial trust from the oil industry of the North Atlantic. In the oil industry's absence, Shetland has been able to invest in other business ventures in balancing its economy.

As discussed earlier, the responsibility for the planning and implementation of sound, ethical ecotourism programmes should fall on the shoulders of regional and national authorities. However, both tourists and operators must also accept some of this responsibility. Accordingly, from the tourist's perspective, he or she must demand certain basic requirements that will ensure a high-quality and ethical experience. These requirements include the following:

(1) Are local people employed in the operation of the business?

(2) Are local people in middle or upper management of the firm?

(3) Is respect shown for indigenous/local people?

(4) Is respect shown for the wildlife of the region, and what precautions are taken to ensure this?

(5) How is the operation economically beneficial to local people?

(6) Does the operation use green hotels, restaurants, transportation, etc.? Question the type of sewage and waste management.

(7) The degree of environmental education delivered in the product?

(8) Number of participants in the tour group?

(9) Level of experience and education of field guides?

(10) Language barriers to communication, if applicable?

(11) Has the tour operator extensive knowledge of the trip (i.e. has the operator been to the site before, and how many times)?

(12) How much pre-trip and trip information is provided to ecotourists?

(13) Contribution to conservation, either financially or physically (planting trees or removing garbage)?

(14) How in touch is the operator with local land use and park management policies (guidelines, regulations)?

In summary, the question from Burroughs at the outset of this chapter makes reference to the fact that we live in a superficial and valueless world. As a major global economic force, tourism is caught in the mainstream of a complex civilisation that tends to emphasise material ends over other, more virtuous ends. As part of the tourism industry, ecotourism will have to struggle to identify itself as part of either the conventional front or the alternative front. The coming years will thus be important in defining just what 'alternative' means, and the role that ecotourism plays in building a better alternative. If it is more about false burdens, vanities, and artificial wants, then ecotourism, I submit, will not be successful in its true meaning. If, on the other hand, it demands a values-based approach in philosophy and application, then indeed it will have something to contribute to human-human and human environment relationships and, in doing so, may act as a model for other forms of development–tourism and non tourism–in a very complex world.